THE PRAYER OF FAITH

THE PRAYER OF FAITH

By

CARRIE JUDD MONTGOMERY

AUTHOR OF
LILIES FROM THE VALE OF THOUGHT AND
ZAIDA EVERSEY OR LIFE TWO-FOLD

Printed in the United States of America and Australia.

Bottom of the Hill Publishing
Memphis, TN
www.BottomoftheHillPublishing.com

ISBN: 978-1-61203-383-9

"Is any sick among you? let him call for the elders of the church; and let them pray over him, anointing him with oil in the name of the Lord: And the prayer of faith shall save the sick, and the Lord shall raise him up; and if he have committed sins, they shall be forgiven him." — JAMES 5:14, 15.

WHO ARE TOILING ON WITH SCARCE STRENGTH TO LIFT THEIR BURDENS; AND TO THOSE WHOSE WORK HAS LONG BEEN LAID ASIDE, WHO LIE ON BEDS OF SICKNESS IN NOISELESS, DARKENED ROOMS; TO THE LOVED ONES EVERYWHERE, WHO ARE WORN WITH WEARINESS AND PAIN, WITH A PRAYER THAT IT MAY BRING TO EACH AND ALL WHO READ IT, THE FAITH AND HOPE WHICH WILL INSPIRE THEM TO SEEK FOR HEALTH OF BODY, AND GREATER STRENGTH OF SOUL, FROM CHRIST, THE GREAT PHYSICIAN

CONTENTS

ADDED NOTES OF PRAISE PREFACE; TO EDITION OF 1894

In publishing a new edition of this little book, I find it in my heart to add a few notes of grateful praise for God's wondrous keeping power in my life since He first restored me to health in answer to the prayer of faith.

I can scarcely find words expressive enough to describe the remarkable degree of strength which has been vouchsafed to me by my blessed Healer during all these years. My exceedingly delicate constitution has seemed to be changed to one of iron, so that I have endured the most arduous and continuous labors without exhaustion. Especially has this wondrous strength been noticeable in the severe test which has been brought to bear upon my nerves in the constant pressure of brain work which has been necessitated by my immense correspondence with the sick, my editorial duties in connection with publishing my monthly Journal, Triumphs of Faith, and the very great call for sympathy in all the cases of sickness and suffering which are continually brought to my notice. I have been entirely relieved from the slightest tendency to the awful headaches with which I constantly suffered before and during my prolonged illness so that after a hard day of intellectual labor I have not even experienced the slightest brain weariness. All this has been the effect, I am fully persuaded, of the blessed indwelling of the Spirit of Life, who has quickened my mortal body, and made it His temple. (Rom. 8:11)

Sometimes, when there has been a little turning aside, a little failure to hearken and obey the dear Holy Spirit, there has been a temporary failure of this marvelous strength, but the quick confession and restoration of perfect communion through the blood of Jesus, has brought again the flow of His healing life.

Since writing this little book, many changes have come into my life, chief among these my marriage with my dear husband, and removal of my work from Buffalo, N. Y., to his home in California. My dear husband is perfectly one with me in all my work for the blessed Master, and together we have proved the truth of the text, that though "one chase a thousand," "two shall put ten thousand to flight."

I add to this testimony a little account which my husband has written of his conversion, and marvelous healing of Diabetes, in answer to the prayer of faith. God has given, us a little daughter, Faith Judd Montgomery, who was also suddenly healed by the Great Physician when apparently at the point of death. We cannot find words to praise God for His bountiful goodness and mercy.

My Home of Peace, a continuation of my Faith Rest, which I had for several years in Buffalo, N. Y., is now located at Beulah, Alameda County, Cal. Beulah is not yet to be found on the map, as it is a little temperance town which my husband and I are starting on consecrated ground, and so far it is composed wholly of Christians. It is situated among the beautiful hills of Laundry Farm, not far from Mills College, and five miles from Oakland, and can be reached by the California Railway which connects at Fruitvale with Oakland local trains. We are always glad to have friends visit the work on Friday, which is my day at home.

Since this book was written, we have seen God's power manifested in the healing of hundreds who have been past all human aid, and we have seen these restored lives laid joyfully upon the altar, and used wondrously in God's service. How full of blessing are our lives when we do not limit the Holy One of Israel by our unbelief.

In closing, we would also praise God for the great good which He has been pleased to accomplish through this little book, not only here in America, but also in its English, German, French, Swedish, and Dutch editions. As we send out this new American edition, making it lower in price than ever soul, and my one aim has been to live to the glory of God, and to win precious souls for Him.

For several years I had suffered greatly from ill-health, and had continually traveled and consulted with physicians hoping to find some remedy. My constitution had been completely broken through fevers contracted in Mexico, and my life of fashionable dissipation had added to my physical troubles, until at last I was beyond all human hope with Diabetes. I tried all kinds of remedies but to no avail. I felt a little benefited during my trip to Japan, but after my return grew worse, and the doctors told me I had but a short time to live. I was quite resigned to die, because I was resting in the finished work of Christ. I did not know anything about Divine Healing until one of my physicians in San Francisco came to me and related some marvelous cures which had taken place among some of his patients, in answer to prayer. This physician was a Christian, and he was convinced that it must be the hand of God which had healed these people, because they were past all human power. Among others, his wife and sister had been healed. I did not believe very much, for I thought that the days of miracles were past. But he came again, and brought many passages of Scripture which bore upon the subject, and asked me to look them up and read them for myself. I had thought that the Doctor was being carried away with some "strange doctrine," like Christian Science or. Spiritualism (which, I am convinced, are both of the Devil) but when he gave me these Scripture texts, I saw for myself that God has promised to be the Physician of His people, if they will trust Him. I read such texts as, Ex. 15:26; Ex. 23:25; Deut. 7:15; Jas. 5:14, 15; Mark 11:24, and many others, diligently comparing Scripture with Scripture, asking the Holy Spirit to be my Teacher and show me what these texts meant. The light began to dawn upon me, and I saw that I had no more foundation in God's Word for the salvation of my soul, than I had for the healing of my body. I saw that it was unbelief which kept God's children from accepting this blessing which He was so willing to bestow upon them. I knew that " Faith cometh by hearing, and hearing by the Word of God," so I studied God's Word more and more and faith increased accordingly. I also attended some meetings on this subject, which were then being held by Rev. J. A. Dowie in Oakland, and I heard remarkable testimonies from many who had been healed of incurable diseases in answer to prayer. My faith continued to increase and I realized that Jesus Christ is "the same yesterday and to-day and forever." Finally, prayer was offered for and with me, and, as we are commanded to do in Mark xi: 24, I believed then and there that I did receive. I had no special manifestation at the time, but believed that I was made "every whit whole " by the power of God. The next morning I realized the new life which had been imparted, and felt as though I could run like a boy, although before this I had been scarcely able to walk up the stairs. I had been living on diet recommended by my physicians, which contained no starch or sugar, but now I began to eat everything, taking God's blessing upon it, and knowing that it made no difference what I ate, because I was every whit made whole.

Health and strength returned, and I was not only healed of Diabetes, but also of chronic rheumatism, which had troubled me for many years and had greatly crippled me at times. My nervous system which had been completely shattered was restored. My life is now one continued psalm of praise.

"I have learned the wondrous secret,
Of abiding in the Lord:
I have found the strength and sweetness
Of confiding in His word;
I have tasted Life's pure fountain,
I am drinking of His blood,
I have lost myself in Jesus,
I am sinking into God.

"All my sicknesses I bring Him,
And He bears them all away;
All my fears and griefs I tell Him,
All my cares from day to day,
All my strength I draw from Jesus,
By His breath I live and move;
E'en His very mind He gives me,
And His faith, and life, and love.

"For my words I take His wisdom,
For my works His Spirit's power,
For my ways His ceaseless Presence,
Guards and guides me every hour.
Of my heart He is the portion,
Of my joy the boundless spring,
Saviour, Sanctifier, Healer,
Glorious Lord and coming King."
THE PRAYER OF FAITH.

CHAPTER I
MARVELOUS HEALING IN
ANSWER TO PRAYER

No, 60 CONNECTICUT STREET,
BUFFALO, N. Y., July 9th, 1880.

ON the sixth of January, 1877, after a gradual decline in health, I was prostrated with an attack of fever, proceeding from my spine, the result, probably, of a severe fall on a stone sidewalk several months before. The fever was soon subdued, but my disease grew into settled spinal difficulty, and from the inflammation of the spinal nerves proceeded a most distressing hyper-acuteness, called hyperesthesia. This extended to all my large joints; and my hips, knees and ankles could not be touched even by myself, on account of their sensitiveness. The disease increased until the nerves in the joints were so unnaturally alive that it was as if they had been laid bare, and it seemed to line as though nothing less than spasms would be the immediate result were they touched. The vibrating of these sensitive nerves, occasioned by the tiniest jar or noise in the room, was something indescribably dreadful.

For all but the first two months of my illness, extreme helplessness as well as suffering made my lot almost unendurable. For more than two years, turning over alone or moving myself a particle in bed was simply an impossibility. Every move was made for me with the greatest care. I suffered intensely with my head; the violent, tearing pain, the terrible sense of weight, and the extreme sensitiveness made a soft, small pillow feel like a block of stone, the pressure of which was crushing my brain to atoms. Much of the time we were obliged to exclude from the room all excepting those who had the care of me.

For eleven months I could not sit up at all, but in the spring of 1878 improved slowly, and could be lifted into a chair for a little while each day. I was more comfortable until July, but I could not by my greatest exertions get able to help myself at all. The only way in which I could be moved from the bed to the chair, was by being lifted under my arms, as I could endure no pressure on my spine.

The very warm weather at that time, and my making attempts to help myself when in such a weak condition, caused a sudden and violent relapse, and, in spite of everything that could be done for me, I continued to fail. I rallied a little in the autumn, but only temporarily.

In January, 1879, my mother's mother, who had lived with us for years and who was very dear to me, died at our house, after a short illness. I was so low at the time, that there could be no public notice of her death, and only a few intimate friends were admitted into our silent house.

By the middle of February, my weakness was so great that most of the time I could scarcely speak in a whisper, and sometimes could only move my lips. Often the exertion of whispering one word would cause the perspiration to start profusely; and I would lie for hours needing something rather than ask for it. I could take no solid food, whatever, and it exhausted me greatly to swallow even liquid food.

My disease had grown into blood consumption; I was emaciated to a shadow, and my largest veins looked like mere threads. Nothing could keep me warm, and the chill of death seemed upon me. A great part of the time I lay gasping faintly for breath, and I suffered excruciatingly. Even the weight of my arms and limbs seemed to be almost unendurable, and this terrible strain was constant. My pulse could scarcely be found, and I was not expected to live from one day to the next. Everything that the most skillful physicians could do for me, had been done; only the "Great Physician" could restore me by His almighty power. I have no doubt that it was ordered by Providence, that, just at this time, there should appear in the daily paper a short account of the wonderful cures performed in answer to the prayers of Mrs. Edward Mix, a colored lady, of Wolcottville, Conn. The article represented her as an earnest, humble Christian, who simply professed to be doing God's work. She had, herself, been cured after years of ill health, by the prayers and laying on of hands of a Rev. Mr. Allen, of Springfield. Mother mentioned these facts to me, and the more I thought on the subject, the more I felt that a letter must be written her in regard to my own case. I had often heard of faith-cures before this, and there had been read to me some portions of W. W. Patton's book, "Remarkable Answers to Prayer," but, although not discrediting them, none had ever produced so great an impression on my mind as this short account of Mrs. Mix. I waited a few hours, then requested my sister to write her that I believed her great faith might avail for me, if she would pray for my recovery, even if she were not present to lay her hands upon me. On Tuesday, February 25th, her answer came as follows:

WOLCOTTVILLE, CONN., February 24th, 1879.
Miss CARRIE JUDD:
I received a line from your sister Eva, stating your case, your disease and your faith. I can encourage you, by the Word of God. that "according to your faith" so be it unto you; and besides you have this promise, "The prayer of faith shall save the sick, and the Lord shall raise him up." Whether the person is present or absent, if it is a "prayer of faith" it is all the same, and God has promised to raise up the sick ones, and if they have committed sins to forgive them. Now this promise is to you, as if you were the only person living. Now if you can claim that promise, I have not the least doubt but what you will be healed. You will first have to lay aside all medicine of every description. Use no remedies of any kind for anything. Lay aside trusting in the "arm of flesh," and lean wholly upon God and His promises. When you receive this letter I want you to begin to pray for faith, and Wednesday afternoon the female prayer-meeting is at our house. We will make you a subject of prayer, between the hours of three and four. I want you to pray for yourself, and pray believing and then act faith. It makes no difference how you feel, but

get right out of bed and begin to walk by faith. Strength will come, disease will depart and you will be made whole. We read in the Gospel, "Thy faith hath made thee whole." Write soon.

Yours in faith,
MRS. EDWARD MIX.

Is it any wonder that in my utter weakness, my confirmed helplessness, and, above all, my lack of faith, that I was tempted to smile unbelievingly at the words "get right out of bed and begin to walk by faith "? My conscience reproved fine for my unbelief, and I began to pray for an increase of faith. I left off all medicine at once, though I confess it was with a struggle, for I was very dependent upon it for temporary alleviation of my extreme suffering. At the hour appointed by Mrs. Mix, members of our own family also offered up prayer, though not in my room. Just before this, I seemed to have no power, whatever, to grasp the promise. Terrible, darkness and powerful temptations from Satan rose to obscure even the little faith I had, but, suddenly, my soul was filled with a childlike peace and confidence, different from anything I had ever before experienced.

There was no excitement, but, without the least fear or hesitation, I turned over and raised up alone, for the first time in over two years. My nurse, Mrs. H., who had taken care of me for nearly a year, was greatly affected, and began praising God for His wonderful power and mercy.

Directly after, with a little support from my nurse, I walked a few steps to my chair. During that same hour, a decided change was perceptible in my color, circulation and pulse, and I could talk aloud with ease. Referring to my diary, which was kept by Mrs. H., I find under February 27 th, which was the day after my restoration: "Carrie moved herself in bed several times during the night. This afternoon she walked from her chair to the bed, a distance of about eight feet, by taking hold of my arms. The Lord strengthens her every hour, both physically and in faith. Blessed be His holy Name!" Then, under February 28th: "Carrie grows stronger,-

moves herself more easily-, rests better nights, has a good appetite. I gave her a sponge-bath this afternoon, and I could not but notice the change in the color of her flesh; instead of the yellow, dead look, it is pink and full of life." Under March 1st: "This morning she drew on her stockings." March 2nd: "Her chest and lungs have been strong; she has talked aloud a great deal. Appetite good; color fresh and clear."

In about three weeks I could walk around the room without even having any one near me; in four weeks I walked down stairs with a little assistance; I walked very steadily from the first, and my joints, which had been so weakened by the hyperesthesia, grew strong and firm at once. My muscles filled out very rapidly, but I suffered nothing from aching or lameness, even after I commenced going up and down stairs.

The first pleasant day in April I went out of doors and into a neighbor's. It seemed as though it was almost too much joy to comprehend, to really be out in the air and sunshine once more. I looked up at the windows of my room with a vague idea that there must be imprisoned there still, a prostrate, suffering creature, of whom I had once been a part, but now was freed from by some mysterious process. The thought of my long and terrible suffering, and of my sudden and joyful deliverance, almost overwhelms me now as I review it all so minutely.

I will mention here, that it was especially noticeable, during my healing, that whenever I made any extra exertion of my own, suddenly, and without the least apparent cause, my strength would fail me. It was soon revealed to me, that I was simply to look to the Lord for improvement; that as He had begun the work, He would carry it on without any strivings on my part.

The more fully I cast myself upon Him, the more I was supported, and often I felt borne up as if by some buoyancy in the air, while there was little or no effort of my own. Even more wonderful, and infinitely more precious, than being brought from death unto life, physically, is the renewed life which the soul experiences at the same time under the healing influence of the Holy Spirit. A deep, intense love for God is implanted in the heart, worldly desires and ambitions sink into nothingness, the one absorbing thought is to be conformed more and more to the image of Christ, and the forgiveness of sins promised with the healing in James 5:14, 15, is experienced as never before.

My gain in flesh and strength was rapid, and my friends say that I am now looking better than ever before. The trouble in my head, which was almost constant for a long time before my prostration, entirely disappeared when I was cured, and I can do a vast amount of studying and writing without even a slight headache. I can also take very long walks and enjoy them.

I wish to add that Dr. Charles Cullis, of Boston, Mass., whose faith-works and faith cures are so widely known, kindly added his prayers for my complete recovery.

All glory be to our merciful and loving Redeemer! and that I may ever abide in Him, and bring forth the "fruit of the Spirit," is the daily prayer of my life.

CARRIE F. JUDD.

With my kind pastor's permission I publish the following letter; his reply to one which I received from a stranger:

No. 790 SEVENTH STREET, BUFFALO, N. Y., March 11th, 1880.

DEAR SIR: Miss Judd has shown me your favor and requests me to vouch for her entire credibility.

I do this with great pleasure, the more so that I have known her so long, and have been entirely conversant with all the facts in the case, from the beginning. I can assure you of her long and painful illness, of her utter and complete prostration, of the immediate expectation of death by herself and all her friends; during all those months I ministered at her bedside, and saw her draw nearer and nearer to the end.

But suddenly, and, of course, by the interposition of God, and doubtless in answer to the prayers of the Church, and of the faithful, she was, so to speak, in a day restored, and is now in perfect health. Of these facts I assure you. They are well known to all here, and you have only to ask any resident of Buffalo to be satisfied of the truthfulness of all that she may tell you.

Why should it be accounted strange that God should raise one of His children from the bed of death? I confess I see no reason. His promise was for all time, "unto you, and to your children," and if we gain less now, it is because we are less faithful, and not because His promise is less sure.

I shall be glad to give you any further information in my power, if you desire it. Very truly,

C. F. A. BIELBY,

Rector St. Mary's-Church-on-the-Hill (Episcopal).

NOTE —Rev. Mr. Bielby is not at present Rector of St. Mary's Church.

CHAPTER II
THE POWER
OF JESUS' NAME

I BELIEVE that the command comes to me, as it came to that restored and rejoicing man so many hundred years ago: "Go home to thy friends and tell them how great things the Lord hath done for thee, and hath had compassion on thee." — St. Mark 5:19. A precious thought it is to me, that, in the strong bond of fellowship and love which exists between Christ's disciples, I may know you all as friends. So home to each one of you I would come, with the peculiar tenderness and sympathy which suffering draws forth from those who have suffered likewise, and I long to speak words of comfort, which will assure you that there is "balm in Gilead," and a "Physician there."

It is with this end in view that I have related, in the foregoing chapter, my experience of the Divine healing power, which has given me renewed life, spiritual and physical.

How strange and sad it is that when the Bible abounds in such rich promises for supplying the need both of soul and body, that we should be languishing in either. Let us together, earnestly and prayerfully, search God's Word, and by its light dispel the mists of unbelief, which prevent our seeing clearly the blessings which are only awaiting our grasp of faith.

We are not apt to accept the Bible as literally as we ought. We get into a dangerous habit of considering its exhortations as in a great degree figurative or sacredly poetic, or as relating to past generations and not to our own. It is no wonder, therefore, if we read our Guide of Life in a way so erroneous, that we get into very loose notions respecting our duties in obeying it.

If we would accept every command contained in the Bible, as a direct command to us from our Lord, and obey them all as literally as they are intended to be obeyed, we should find inestimable blessings attending such a course. Having had light and grace given me to determine to do this, I have found that it is only needful for me to make the effort to obey, and the strength to do so comes immediately from a higher source.

None of the Lord's injunctions are too difficult to obey, if we make the effort trusting in His strength, and who of us, that have kept the Lord's commandments, have not found that "in keeping of them there is great reward"? — Psa. 19:11.

Let us look at the literal command which the inspired apostle gives concerning the sick. He says, "Is any sick among you? let him call for the elders of the church; and let them pray over him, anointing him with oil in the name of the Lord: And the prayer of faith shall save the sick, and the Lord shall raise him up; and if he have committed sins, they shall be forgiven him." — James 5:14, 15.

This is certainly not a grievous command, and yet how willing we are to go to every trouble and expense before following these simple and plain directions. Have they seemed to some of us, as seemed the instructions of Elisha to Naaman, the leper,—too simple and easy to think of obeying? If so, let us remember the words of Naaman's servants, who "came near, and spoke unto him, and said, My father, if the prophet had bid thee do some great thing, wouldest thou not have done it? how much rather then, when he saith to thee, Wash, and be clean?"

In St. Mark i: 32, occur these words: "And at even, when the sun did set, they brought unto Him all that were diseased;" and again in St. Luke iv: 40, we read: "Now when the sun was setting, all they that had any sick with divers diseases brought them unto Him; and He laid His hands on every one of them, and healed them." Both St. Mark and St. Luke allude in these passages to the fact of its being evening and the time of the setting sun, and this seems to figuratively illustrate the fact that only in the evening of human hope were they willing to go to Christ for peace and healing. And why do we wait until the glare of disappointing earthly suns has passed away, before we are ready to perceive the soothing, lovely light of the " Sun of Righteousness," which unto those who fear God's name, shall "arise with healing in His wings."

With the promise in James so plain before us, it is strange and sad that we should languish so long on beds of suffering, making no effort to claim this promised healing; and why ?— let us consider some of the difficulties which are shutting out so many of us from a full enjoyment of our privileges.

A great obstacle which meets us at the outset, is the sad unbelief of the world, and, sadder still, of many professed Christians. When the fainting hope of some suffering one is revived by a prayerful reading of the gracious promises in the Bible, that hope is often shattered by some friend who says rebukingly: "O, you cannot be healed in that way. Miracles long ago ceased."

What matters it to our readily deceived hearts, that we can find nothing in the Bible to support this assertion?—we suppose that the world must be right about it, and so we believe the word of our fellow-creatures, and make "the Word of God of none effect" through these traditions. — St. Mark 7:13.

A great and good man, who is widely known all over the United States, wrote to a friend, concerning the subject of faith-healing: "With the open Book before me, I do not see why these things cannot be." It is because we do not keep our eyes closely enough fixed on our open Bibles that we fail to "behold wondrous things out of God's law." Can we say with David: "O, how I love Thy law! it is my meditation all the day"?

It is written in Acts 2:39, "For the promise is 'unto you, and to your children, and to all that are afar off.'" St. Peter is speaking, of the gift of the Holy Ghost, and none who have felt the wonderful power, which, in answer to the "prayer of faith," gives healing to soul and body, can doubt that it is the power of the Holy Spirit, promised to all ages and generations. There are many who refuse to give credence to faith-cures, because, as they strenuously assert, "the age of miracles is past." What authority they can give for this statement, remarkable as it is when so many miracles, spiritual and physical, are being performed by the power of the Holy Spirit, every day, we leave them to tell; but we would press the inquiry upon them—if these marvelous cures are not wrought by God, by what power are they performed? Some would attribute them to "physical phenomena," " influence of mind over mind," "faith cooperating with the faculties of volition," etc., but when we present for their investigation, well-authenticated cases where cancers, tumors, consumption, and other fatal diseases are cured in a wonderfully short time in answer to the " prayer of faith," when—as in a case which Dr. Cullis relates in his introduction to the book "Dorothea Trudel" —broken bones unite in less than twenty-four hours because of a little child's faith, then their reasons cannot seem plausible to the most prejudiced minds.

They must either stubbornly refuse to believe in these cases of healing without giving any reasons for their unbelief; or else rightfully ascribe them to Divine power; or (and I shudder at the thought of any one's committing such blasphemy) attribute them to diabolical agency.

There were those who attributed to Satan, even the miracles which Christ performed while on the earth. The Pharisees said: *'This fellow doth not cast out devils but by Beelzebub, the prince of devils." Let us remember Christ's answer, and beware lest we make any approach to that terrible and unpardonable sin, which shall not be forgiven men "neither in this world, neither in the world to come." "Wherefore I say unto you that all manner of sin and blasphemy shall be forgiven unto men: but the blasphemy against the Holy Ghost shall not be forgiven unto men." — St. Matt, 12:31.

Immediately after this rebuke our Saviour adds: "Either make the tree good and his fruit good; or else make the tree corrupt and his fruit corrupt: for the tree is known by his fruit." Let us pause a moment to ask what fruit is brought forth in the lives of those who have experienced these "miracles of healing."

Do we see these restored people rushing into vanity and

sin, using their renewed health and strength in the service of the devil? Far from it! We see them consecrating every power of soul and body to loving, joyful service for their Lord and Master; we see them a "peculiar people, zealous of good works," desirous of following as closely as possible the footsteps of their Saviour.

The man whose sight had been restored, said to the Pharisees when speaking of Jesus: "Why herein is a marvelous thing, that ye know not from whence He is, and yet He hath opened mine eyes. Now we know that God heareth not sinners: but if any man be a worshiper of God, and doeth His will, him He heareth," and we may say likewise that it would indeed be a "marvelous thing " if devoted Christians, who give their lives entirely to the Lord, are servants of the devil.

Dr. Charles Cullis, through whose "prayer of faith " so many sufferers have been healed, says: "'I have noticed in every case of healing by prayer, as great a blessing has come to the soul as to the body. This has been invariable." And why should it not be so, when we are told that if the sick person has "committed sins they shall be forgiven him "? Whoever takes it upon himself to rebuke those who perform miracles in the name of Jesus Christ, will do well to read our Saviour's own words on this subject: "And John answered Him, saying, Master, we saw one casting out devils in Thy name, and he followeth not us; and we forbade him, because he followeth not us. But Jesus said, Forbid him not, for there is no man which shall do a miracle in My name, that can lightly speak evil of Me. For he that is not against us is on our part." — St. Mark 9:38-40. In My name, Christ says, and that is the vast difference between the miracles wrought by the power of the Holy Spirit, and those false wonders performed in the name of the Virgin or at the shrines of other saints.

St. Peter, filled with the Holy Ghost, said unto the " rulers of the people, and elders of Israel," " If we this day be examined of the good deed done to the impotent man, by what means he is made whole; be it known unto you all that by the name of Jesus Christ of Nazareth, Whom ye crucified, Whom God raised from the dead, even by Him doth this man stand here before you whole. Neither is there salvation in any other: for there is none other name under Heaven given among men whereby we must be saved." — Acts 4:9, 10, 12.

That false miracles could not be performed in the name of Christ was proven by the terrible experience of the unconverted Jews, related in Acts 19:13, 15, 16.

"Then certain of the vagabond Jews, exorcists, took upon them to call over them which had evil spirits, the name of the Lord Jesus, saying, We adjure you by Jesus whom Paul preacheth. And the evil spirit answered and said, Jesus I know, and Paul I know; but who are ye? And the man in whom the evil spirit was, leaped on them, and overcame them, and prevailed against them, so that they fled out of that house, naked and wounded."

In Christ's parting commission to His disciples He mentions, among other signs that shall follow those who believe, "they shall lay hands on the sick and they shall recover," but notice that all of these wonderful things were to be done in Christ's name: "In My name shall they cast out devils."

O, let us not refuse to recognize the power of our Redeemer's name, and when we cry for mercy to that blessed Saviour, let us, like blind Bartimeus, persist until our calls reach His gracious ear. There are many sweet and comforting lessons in this account of the healing of Bartimeus, if we read it with understanding.

"And it came to pass, that as He was come nigh unto Jericho, a certain blind man sat by the wayside begging." How in our spiritual blindness we all sit " by the wayside begging"— asking paltry alms of those who are unwilling, and, again, of those who are unable, of their own poverty, to give—when if we would but seek Jesus, we should receive with Him the fullness of all blessing. "He that spared not His own Son, but delivered Him up for us all, how shall He not with Him freely give us all things?"

This man heard the tread of the multitude, and he asked what it meant, "And they told him that Jesus of Nazareth passeth by." Happy are we if we are not spiritually deaf as well as blind; for many there be who will not listen to the sound of the footsteps of those who follow Christ, "lest," as the Lord says, "they should be converted and I should heal them." But if we are ready and willing to ask what these things mean, we shall not fail of receiving the answer, "Jesus of Nazareth passeth by."

Then our cry, like that of blind Bartimeus, will arise above all of their tumult, "Jesus, Thou Son of David, have mercy on me." And they which went before, rebuked him, that he should hold his peace; just as many who go before, or occupy the first place in Christian churches nowadays, take it upon themselves to rebuke those who seek for Christ's healing mercy. If many of the ministers or "elders" of the present day had lived at that time and heard the blind man's cries, they would doubtless have represented to him the exceeding sinfulness of seeking to be delivered from an infirmity which he ought simply to bear with resignation.

O, how we limit the power and mercy of the Great Shepherd! How unwilling we are to accept what God, of His exceeding goodness, is so willing to give!

But Bartimeus' faith in Christ's mercy was much greater than his fear of those who rebuked him, and "he cried so much the more, Thou Son of David have mercy on me." If he had only listened to the reproving voices of those who went before, and had not persisted in turning from them to Jesus Himself, how great the blessing he must have forfeited.

Did Jesus pass by that blind man with a rebuking word and a command to submit patiently to his affliction? Ah, no! for was not that merciful Saviour Himself willing to bear, in his own body, the sins and sorrows of the blind man, and of all those who will by faith cast their burden upon the cross?

We hear His voice in kindness and power, "What wilt thou that I shall do unto thee?" Think what these words would mean coming even from an earthly monarch; how much more do they convey spoken by Him to whom "all power has been given in heaven and in earth."

"What wilt thou?"—we may each one of us hear this question from our Lord, and as many of His promises as we choose to accept by faith, will be made real to us.

The blind man's request was that he might receive his sight. He was then capable of understanding only the blessing of having the darkness removed from his physical vision, but with Jesus' words, "Receive thy sight, thy faith hath saved thee," his soul also received new powers of vision, and he joyfully beheld the "True Light" Who hath said, "I am the light of the world: he that followeth Me shall not walk in darkness, but shall have the light of life."

"And immediately he received his sight, and followed Him glorifying God: and all the people when they saw it gave praise unto God." It is recorded of this man, as of so many others who were healed by Christ, that his first act, after being made whole, was to glorify God. Adoration is the essential outpouring of the heart which recognizes its Redeemer, who "Himself took our infirmities, and bare our sicknesses." — St. Matt, 8:17.

And, like David, we may sing with joyful lips, "Bless the Lord, O! my soul, and forget not all His benefits: who forgiveth all thine iniquities; who healeth all thy diseases."

CHAPTER III
THE NATURE OF FAITH

I TRUST that there are many of you, my dear friends, who, clinging closely to the word of God instead of to the traditions of men, are already beginning to realize the blessed privilege which may be yours—that of accepting your Saviour as the Great Physician" of your soul and body.

You may answer that you long ago accepted Him as the Physician of your soul; but do you really feel satisfied that you have experienced a complete spiritual healing? Are you fully assured that your sins are forgiven, and that your soul has been born anew? Do you feel that you have been brought to the full salvation, which Christ meant should be ours, when He suffered on Calvary? I doubt not that there are many hearts that will give sad answers to these questions, knowing, as they do, that they have not been "filled with joy and with the Holy Ghost." — Acts 13:52.

I beg of you then to trust God for a more complete healing of soul than you have ever known before, and trust Him, also, for the healing of your weak, suffering body. I think I can tell, from my own experience, one of the first temptations which you will encounter in your attempt to do this. You are probably saying: "Other people may claim the promise in Jas. 5:14, 15, but I am not good enough. God would not thus favor any but those who had led very holy lives."

We are so apt to lose sight of the all-important fact that we have no righteousness of our own, that "there is none righteous; no, not one," but we may, and must, put on Christ, as our righteousness. We all know this; but do we all realize it? Considering our own unworthiness, we have none of us a right to present a single petition to God. "For there is no difference; for all have sinned, and come short of the glory of God." — Rom. 3:22, 23.

It is one of Satan's delusions, that even while we are thus holding back, from a sense of our sinfulness, we are consoled for our lack of faith by a half-conscious acknowledgment of what we think is our humility.

The right kind of humility is indeed very necessary; but we must look entirely away from self, to our Saviour, and thus realize what we may receive through His merits. We may "come boldly to the throne of grace" through "the righteousness of God, which is by faith of Jesus Christ unto all, and upon all them that believe."

Clad in the robe of His righteousness, we may then claim all the wonderful blessings extended to the righteous.

We read: "Thou Lord wilt bless the righteous, with favor wilt thou compass him as with a shield;" "The Lord loveth the righteous;" "His secret is with the righteous;" "The desire of the righteous shall be granted;" "The righteous is delivered out of trouble;" "The way of the righteous is made plain;" and many more such precious texts, which, when we realize that they may be ours through Christ, make our hearts sing for joy.

In the examples of great faith, given us in the Gospels, we see how persistently and fearlessly the most humble sinners approached their holy Lord, when losing sight of themselves in Him.

Notice the difference between the conduct of the ten lepers who "stood afar off," and that of the other poor leper we read of, who came to Jesus, "beseeching Him and kneeling down to Him." The former dared not approach Christ, because of the law respecting their terrible disease, but the latter had, it seems, in his importunity and faith, dared to approach so near the Saviour, that He could touch him by putting forth His hand.

So we, viewing ourselves in the light of the law, see our souls so vile and loathsome that we dare not approach the Holy One; ,but when, with the eye of faith, we behold ourselves as already cleansed by the blood of Jesus, we feel no longer our pollution, but are ready to approach Him, and receive " according to our faith."

When we begin to realize that "God is no respecter of persons," and that all who go to Him in the name of Jesus Christ, are accepted alike; when we have given up the idea that any one can have righteousness of his own, then a very great barrier is broken down between God's good gifts and ourselves. But Satan is always ready to set up new barriers, and he comes to us with difficulties concerning our faith.

We are apt to regard faith as something high and mysterious, which no one can attain unless born with an unusual degree of it. Some of us are deceived by thinking that great and repeated struggles of mind are necessary in order to secure it, and this idea is pretty strongly rooted, until we really understand the nature of faith. I could not express this erroneous notion better than by repeating the very remark which a lady made to me not long ago. After questioning me about my cure, she exclaimed: "Well, I'm sure I never could muster up enough faith!"

Faith is belief, and the question is not how much we must believe God's word, but whether we accept it as true or not true; whether we deem it reliable or not reliable. There is no neutral ground between faith and unbelief. Of all Satan's delusions, none, perhaps, are more delusive than the errors he puts into our minds regarding faith. Let us take the Bible definition of the word: "Faith is the substance (margin, confidence) of things hoped for, the evidence of things not seen." — Heb. 11:1.

We know that in human transactions if we have the confidence that we shall have what we are hoping for, we make the same calculations, mentally, at least, that we should if we already had it, and when we place that confidence in One who cannot fail, We really have the substance, itself, of our hopes. Again, if we commission a reliable friend to perform some errand for us, we believe that he will do it, and therefore that belief or faith is the evidence in our mind of things as yet unseen. Before we have the evidence of our senses in regard to the matter, we accept the evidence of faith.

Having faith in God is believing His word without looking at probabilities or possibilities, as humanly viewed; without regarding natural circumstances; without considering any apparent obstacles in the way of His keeping His promises. If every avenue of hope seems closed to our human vision, God can open new ones, and we must trust His word through everything. It is not faith simply to believe when we can see all the workings of Providence; it is faith not to be staggered at any complication of adverse circumstances. "And this is the confidence that we have in Him, that if we ask anything according to His will He heareth us: and if we know that He hear us, whatsoever we ask, we know that we have the petitions that we desired of him." — 1 John 5:14, 15. "And whatsoever ye shall ask in My name, that will I do, that the Father may be glorified in the Son. If ye shall ask anything in My name, I will do it." — St. John 14:13, 14.

We get some valuable knowledge, in regard to faith, from the touching and eloquent recital of the healing of the poor woman, in St. Mark 5:25-34. She had been afflicted with her disease for twelve years, "and had suffered many things of many physicians, and had spent all that' she had, and was nothing bettered, but rather grew worse."

How exactly the language of this verse describes the experience of many poor sufferers nowadays, who having sought relief by every means possible, find themselves in a worse condition than when they first sought their physicians, and who are left without money to pay more doctors' bills, even were they not aware that no human skill could remove or alleviate their sufferings.

Just at the time of her utter discouragement, this woman "heard of Jesus." Perhaps she had heard of His wonderful works before this, but until she had tried every means, and they had failed, she was probably not ready or willing to hear of Him with faith, and this is apt to be the case with us.

This poor woman "when she had heard of Jesus, came in the press behind, and touched His garments. For she said, If I may touch but His clothes, I shall be whole." O, that we might thus press through the crowd of doubts and fears, and let nothing stay us until we have touched the hem of Christ's garment!

What, in this poor sufferer's case, was the inevitable result of that touch of faith?" She felt in her body that she was healed of that plague."

A marked lesson is conveyed in the Saviour's inquiry, "Who touched my clothes?" and the answer which He intended this question to bring forth: "And His disciples said unto Him, Thou seest the multitude thronging Thee, and sayest Thou, who touched Me?"

How significant is this of the multitudes who throng Jesus every day, who draw near to Him in prayer, and yet, like this multitude who "followed Him and thronged Him," draw not near in faith. Some who were in that throng were undoubtedly there out of curiosity; some may have passed near and touched Him as an experiment, or test of His power; and some, even, with prayers on their lips, may have been uttering mockeries which they did not expect, and perhaps did not wish, to have regarded.

The disciples marveled that Christ should say, "Who touched me?" when they knew that each moment His contact with someone was unavoidable; but He alone could discern between the touch of faith and the touch of unbelief.

"And He looked round about to see her that had done this thing." Is it not comforting to know that our blessed Lord, in His tender solicitude for us, will thus take such particular notice of every one who dares reach out the hand of faith to touch His sacred robe?

And what does the sequel teach? That we must not keep silent about the great things which Christ does for us. For His glory we must confess them "before all the people," and then to us, as it did to her, will sound His reassuring voice: "Go in peace."

The physical healing seems to have been given first in this instance, and it was only when she confessed the wondrous work wrought in her, that He gave the "peace which passeth all understanding" to her soul. It may be that we shall be called upon to confess Christ, "with fearing and trembling," as did she; but just as surely He will bid us be of good comfort, and say: "Thy faith hath made thee whole."

Sometimes we cherish the idea that faith is in itself so meritorious that it entitles us to proportionate blessings; but we must keep in mind, that it would make no difference how strong was our belief in God's power, had He not given His Son to die for us, that we might be accepted in Him.

"Thou believest that there is one God; thou doest well; the devils also believe and tremble."—Jas. 2:19. But we must also believe that it is not for our faith's sake, but for Christ's sake alone that we may have all the blessings promised us in His name. Instead of thinking of the merits of faith, we must try to understand how great a sin is unbelief.

We may realize how much we lose by it, but not how criminal it is in the sight of God. If we would look at our unbelieving conduct with the thought that we are representing the faithful God a liar, we should put new force upon the saying: "For whatsoever is not of faith is sin."—Rom. 14:2. "Whatsoever"— this gives us new ideas concerning the sinfulness which we must ask God to forgive; for how much, how very much, there is in all of us, which is "not of faith."

Faith is not meritorious, but it is essential. We must believe fully in God's power, and in His mercy through Christ, in order to put ourselves in a position to receive the desired blessing. Every doubt removes us just so far from claiming the promises; for since faith is laying hold of a blessing, doubt is just the opposite—letting go of it. If we take hold by faith of something we desire, then let go because of doubt, and continue our indecision, doubt generally conquers, and we let go altogether. Having once laid hold of a promise, by faith, we must keep hold of it.

We all have the germ of faith in the power to believe intellectually, but it requires the quickening of the Holy Spirit to change a mere intellectual belief into that living faith by which the promises are made real to us. We must first use the God-given powers of our mind and determine to believe, praying at the same time for the Spirit to enable us to do so. We are told in Gal. v: 22, that faith is the "fruit of the Spirit."

A lady who was cured of a nine-years' blindness, in answer to prayer, wrote to a friend: "I now understand the mystery of the miracles." She had experienced the light and power which had given her new vision, spiritual as well as physical, and could now understand how the faith, "without works and dead," could be renewed and bring forth fruit when quickened by the Spirit.

If we plead in Christ's name for the Comforter, we have full assurance that we shall be answered, for Jesus left us these precious words: "If ye then being evil know how to give good gifts unto your children, how much more shall your Heavenly Father give the Holy Spirit to them that ask Him." We have only to desire and then to ask.

I remember when the wings of faith, my carrier-dove, were so heavy laden with the pollution of my sinful and discouraged soul, that my messages could not arise to Heaven. But were they not, therefore, received of God? Yes, though I knew it not then, He mercifully bent to hear my petitions, though my faith could not arise to Him. The feeblest flutterings of our faith will arouse His tender love, and He will revive and strengthen until it soars trustfully upward.

I will take an extract from Rev. Theo. Monod's writings: "Do you think it would be a great thing—do you think it would be a happy thing for you to give that poor body of yours, that poor heart of yours, to God to live in? Do you think God would accept it? Hear this one word. Jesus Christ says that even as a father will not give a stone for bread to his hungering child, even so—no, He does not say that—He says, 'how much more shall your Heavenly Father give the Holy Spirit'— to them that deserve Him? No! To them that merely keep wishing, for Him? No! To them that ASK for Him. 'Ask and ye shall receive.'"

> "The Shepherd does not ask of thee
> Faith in thy faith, but only faith in Him;
> And this He meant in saying,' Come to Me.'
> In light or darkness seek to do His will,
> And leave the work of faith to Jesus still."

While most of us limit God's mercy, there are others who limit His power. It is strange that any who acknowledge God's omnipotence, can be so inconsistent as to suppose that His power cannot extend to one disease as well as to another, and yet I have heard people specify certain cases, and ask, incredulously, " But do you think that they could be cured in that way?

The prophet says: "Ah, Lord God! behold, Thou hast made the heaven and the earth, by Thy great power and stretched-out arm, and there is nothing too hard for Thee."

Many who seek this healing as a last resort, have very little faith that their cases are within reach of the "Great Physician's" power, and to them a wonderful lesson is presented in the account of healing given in Mark 9:17-30.

The father of the afflicted child had taken him to the disciples to be healed by them, but he found that they were unable to cast out the devil. What little faith the man had possessed, was evidently weakened by their failure, and it was almost in despair that he spoke these words to Jesus, "But if Thou canst do anything, have compassion on us and help us." Do not many of us go with this feeling in our hearts, "Lord, if Thou canst do anything, have compassion on us"?

But Jesus gently rebukes this lack of faith, and proceeds to instruct him in what spirit he must approach Him, if he would have his child cured.

"Jesus said unto him, If thou canst believe, all things are possible to him that believeth." Let us stop a moment to consider the two glorious possibilities, "with God all things are possible," and "all things are possible to him that believeth."

How many of us, judging from our own faithless conduct, would have replied that we did not know how to believe, that we could not believe, that we were not born with faith and were, therefore, incapable of believing.

Did that troubled, sorrowing father answer in this way? Ah, no! he knew the urgency of his son's case; he knew that the only condition was believing, and, without searching his heart to see if he found there some mysterious emotion, such as many people now understand faith to be, he at once signified his willingness to fulfill the necessary condition by making the effort to believe.

"And straightway the father of the child cried out and said, with tears, Lord, I believe, help Thou mine unbelief." Straight-way, without waiting a moment, even while with tears he was bemoaning his lack of faith and asking Christ to help his unbelief, he made the effort of intellect and will, and said, "Lord, I believe."

Not—" Lord I will believe when Thou dost help mine unbe-lief," but—" I will believe, I do believe this moment."

He had acted upon the determination to believe in spite of himself, in spite of his unbelief, and as he made the effort the poiver was given him.

CHAPTER IV
GOD'S BLESSED WILL
FOR HIS CHILDREN

THERE are some dear suffering ones who think they may not claim this promised healing, because it might not be the Lord's will for them to be cured. That God has a wise purpose in allowing sickness to come upon us, we may be certain. He doubtless uses it as one means of the loving chastening, with which he afflicts His children; and to understand better why God chastens us, let us look at Heb. 12:11. "Now no chastening for the present seemeth to be joyous, but grievous; nevertheless, afterward, it yieldeth the peaceable fruit of righteousness unto them which are exercised thereby."

In every providence it is the design of our loving Father to bring us nearer to Himself; to melt our stubborn wills until they may blend with His will, which is all love for us, and to cause us to yield ourselves, souls and bodies, "a living sacrifice, holy, acceptable unto the Lord."

Some may harbor the idea that God is very reluctant to remove suffering from us—that He is- a hard Master who* will only relieve us when we have wearied Him with our importunity; but if is often because we have strayed from our tender Shepherd, that He in mercy afflicts us, and it is because we are so unwilling to return, that the trial must needs continue so long with some of us.

There are other souls who are already near their Saviour, but whose very nearness causes them to catch such precious glimpses of the bliss of being still nearer their loved Redeemer, that they plead with increasing earnestness for this privilege. And these, too, He purines by suffering, until they are freed from the dross which prevents the gold from reflecting His image clearly.

If these suffering ones would yield at once to the Refiner, their unbelief, which represents' the baser metal they had wished destroyed, the trial would quickly end, because no longer needful. And this can be done by faith—by accepting Christ fully and putting all our dependence on Him. We read that the chastening brings forth the "fruit of righteousness," but if we believe fully on Christ we may have His righteousness and a-deliverance from our trial, for "the chastisement of our peace was upon Him, and with His stripes we are healed."

A dear, Christian sister, who was long educated in suffering, wrote me a while ago, "I was honest in my desire to be wholly the Lord's, and nothing so reveals the Divine faithfulness as the very trials which were so deliberate, so protracted, and so thorough. It is strange how much we can endure before we are willing to stop and trust I" "Stop and trust!"—this is just what we must be brought fo, sooner or later, and, as soon as we will, we may obtain deliverance by this means.

I doubt not that our Saviour's loving heart yearns to grant our petitions the moment they are presented, but with what infinite patience and wisdom He waits, that we may be prepared to receive what we have asked of Him, and that will be when we are willing to stop our own endeavors and trust to the work which He has accomplished for us. As much, or as little, as we do this, we receive proportionate blessings, and Jesus has Himself said: "According to your faith be it unto you." This surely means that just as many of the benefits of His atonement as we choose to accept by faith (or belief in Him) may be ours. Would there be any good of soul and body which this would fail to comprehend, if we could grasp His wonderful words in all their fullness? The Psalmist says: "No good thing will He withhold from them who walk uprightly," and when we are walking in Christ, trusting to His full salvation, we are walking uprightly.

While it is a wonderfully blessed truth, that He will not yield to our entreaties before the end so essential to our eternal good is accomplished, it is also just as blessed and true that we may obtain a speedy deliverance out of every trouble, by giving our souls and bodies unreservedly to Him, and resting upon His "full, perfect and sufficient sacrifice" for the sins of the whole world.

I do not mean that no trial will come to us when we have entered upon this life of faith; for, if that were so, how could we understand the blessedness of having such a mighty and conquering Saviour? Just as we must first be convicted of sin to be able to rejoice in being freed from sin, so trials must often come to us that we may taste the joy of knowing that "God is our refuge and strength—a very present help in time of trouble." It is precious to behold what wonderful deliverances He will work for us, even when we seem completely hedged in, if we put our trust in Him.

"O, taste and see that the Lord is good: blessed is the man that trusteth in Him. The young lions do lack and suffer hunger, but they that seek the Lord shall not want any good thing. Many are the afflictions of the righteous, but the Lord delivereth him out of them all." — Psalm 34:8, 10, 19. What wonderful, helpful words, and to think that all the blessedness the Bible tells about, may belong to each and all of us who will claim it through Christ! O, if we would all at this moment "taste and see that the Lord is good." We would only need one taste to make us desire to eat of His goodness evermore, but the trouble is, we will not accept the invitation to even taste.

Jehovah said to Israel, "Open thy mouth wide and I will fill it," but they did not heed; and just so we are crying because of our hunger and will not open our mouths. Hear the loving, grieving words, "O, that my people had hearkened unto me, and Israel had walked in my ways! I should soon have subdued their enemies, and turned my hand against their adversaries." Does that sound as if our Lord rejoiced to see us groaning in affliction? Then He tells with what He would have filled their mouths,—" He should have fed them also with the finest of the wheat, and with honey out of the Rock should I have satisfied thee."

The prophet exhorts to repentance in these words, "Come and let us return unto the Lord, for He hath torn and He will heal us; He hath smitten and He will bind us up." — Hosea. 6:1. And we read in Lamentations 3:32, 33, " But though He cause grief, yet will He have compassion according to the multitude of His mercies. For He doth not afflict willingly, nor grieve the children of men."

And would this tender, loving Father, so much more merciful and loving than it is possible for an earthly parent to be, refuse to deliver us from affliction, when His purpose is accomplished, and we are ready to trust fully to Him?

How plainly are we shown throughout the Bible that it is not the Lord's will to put sickness upon-us, if we will only obey His commands and have faith in His promises. We read, "But if thou shalt indeed obey His voice and do all that I speak, then I will be an enemy unto thy enemies, and an adversary unto thine adversaries; and ye shall serve the Lord your God and I will take sickness away from the midst of thee." — Ex. 23:22, 25.

"Wherefore, it shall come to pass, if ye hearken to these judgments and keep and do them, that the Lord thy God shall keep unto thee the covenant and the mercy which He swore unto thy fathers, and the Lord will take away from thee all sickness, and will put none of the evil diseases of Egypt, which thou knowest, upon thee." — Deut. 7:12, 15.

If we trust fully in Christ's finished work, sin cannot hold us captive, for He "bare our sins in His own body on the tree, that we, being dead to sins, should live unto righteousness." — 1 Peter 2:24.

If we trust fully to His finished work, sickness shall not be able to hold us captive, for Christ " Himself took our infirmities, and bare our sicknesses." — St. Matt, 8:17. And if we trust fully in that finished work, even the grave shall not hold us captive long, for "now is Christ risen from the dead, and become the first fruits of them that slept." — 1 Cor. 15:20.

Sin, sickness and corruption are upon all humanity because of the first Adam's sin; but we may be delivered from sin, sickness and corruption because of the atonement of Christ, "the last Adam." "For as in Adam all die, even so in Christ shall all be made alive." — 1 Cor. 15:22.

O, dear, suffering friends, take the comfort of this, and believe that in Christ you may have every need of soul and body supplied. It is His will that we shall ask Him for both spiritual and physical healing, and, therefore, He has told us by His inspired apostle that "the prayer of faith shall save the sick and the Lord shall raise him up; and if he have committed sins they shall be forgiven him."

In the account of the healing of the leper, in St. Matt, 8:2-4, we see one who had implicit faith in God's power, but who was seeking to know His will. "And behold there came a leper and worshiped Him, saying, Lord, if Thou wilt Thou canst make me clean." If Jesus had, before this, openly proclaimed, as we have since had proclaimed to us through His written Word, that any sick person who asked, believing, would be healed and have his sins forgiven, the man would have gone to Him with different words; for Christ's will in the matter would have been already known to him. He would simply have gone to Him claiming the promise, in words like these: "Lord, I believe that Thou hast power to make me clean, and Thou hast signified Thy willingness to do it."

We think we have a perfect right to take our earthly friends at their word, and to accept promises made by them, and yet we are continually rejecting God's revealed word, and trying to gain for ourselves a peculiar and different revelation.

We must act on our Lord's revealed will, and if we need any further revelation, particularly designed for ourselves, we shall have it clearly and distinctly given us.

Was the Lord's will for that poor leper any different from that which we may know from His written Word, He now wills for us? No, the prayer of faith would save the sick then, and it will now. "And Jesus put forth His hand and touched him, saying, I will; be thou clean, and immediately his leprosy was cleansed."

Now, what is the difference between the case of the poor leper and that of our sick and suffering ones nowadays? The need is the same—healing for the sin-sick soul and body. Then, too, thank God! we have the same "Great Physician" to call to our aid. He is as near us, now, as then He was near the leper; yes, even near enough for His blessed hand to touch us as it did him. The same tender heart, of which we read so often that it was "moved with compassion," is ready, now, to feel for us.

"For we have not a High Priest which cannot be touched with the feeling of our infirmities. Let us, therefore, come boldly unto the throne of grace that we may obtain mercy, and find grace to help in time of need."

The only existing difference between the poor leper's case and our own is, that when he first went to the Saviour he was confident only of His power to heal him, while we, relying on his revealed Word, may have the certainty beforehand, not only of His power but also of His willingness to heal us.

While we must be ready to bow with submission to another revelation if it is made to our souls, we need not be waiting for it; we need not expect it. We may base our confidence on the word He has already given us, and we, too, shall be made "clean." Our flesh shall come again " like unto the flesh of a little child " — 2 Kings 5: 14, and our hearts shall be cleansed with the blood of Jesus.

We read in St. Matt, 4:23: "And Jesus went about all Galilee preaching the gospel of the kingdom and healing all manner of sickness, and all manner of disease among the people." While the tender Physician ministered to the body, taking away pain and disease, and imparting new life to the wasted frame, He was, at the same time, conferring that much more marvelous and precious gift, healing to the sinful, prostrate soul. Those who went to Jesus would not have thought of asking Him to restore their souls, and leave their bodies full of disease. Even those of them who realized, as we so fully realize, that the soul-healing is vastly above anything else in importance, would not have thought of pleading for the greater boon without the less. Why should they, why should we—when Christ is able and willing to give us both?

How surprised and dismayed any of us would be were we to read in the Bible that the leper importuned Christ to heal his sinful soul, and yet added that he could not ask for his leprosy to be cleansed, as that would be too much to ask of Christ. We cannot conceive of the leper's making such a request when within reach of the Saviour's healing touch; and if such a desire were granted him, can we help thinking that, in some respects, the spiritual healing must, of necessity, be imperfect?

And yet we see people whose conduct is precisely like this; who give their hearts into Christ's keeping, but think the healing and keeping of their bodies would be too much to ask of Him, and that they can manage to attend to that, themselves!

That the plague spots on the body, as well as on the heart, were both the effects of the sin from which Christ came to save us, our sinless Saviour knew, and He would not, and did not, extend complete healing to the one and leave the other in bondage.

O, that as many as "have knowledge" of our loving Physician, may do, as did those men in the land of Gennesaret, long ago, who, we read, "sent out into all that country round about, and brought unto Him all that were diseased, and besought Him that they might only touch the hem of His garment, and as many as touched were made perfectly whole."

Let us notice the words which Christ spoke to the poor woman of Canaan, when she pleaded with such humble persistency, for the restoration of her daughter: "Then Jesus answered and said unto her, O, woman, great is thy faith! be it unto thee even as thou wilt. And her daughter was made whole from that very hour."

Whenever, by faith, we approach very near our Lord, we may indeed hear His voice saying, " Be it unto thee even as thou wilt;" for, in that comforting nearness to Him, we are taught His will for our souls and bodies, and, from its very blessedness, we can desire no other. "If ye abide in me, and my words abide in you, ye shall ask what ye will, and it shall be done unto you." — St. John 15: 7. And looking at the verse following this, we learn what is Christ's will for us. "Herein is my' Father glorified, that ye bear much fruit; so shall ye be my disciples."

My friends, judge for yourselves: is it bearing much fruit to continue to be bound by sickness, when, if we would accept the healing so freely offered us, we might work with renewed strength in His vineyard.

May we all strive to understand how beautiful and blessed God's will is for His children, and thus clear away the unbelief with which Satan binds us, in body and soul. Not until we are freed from his chains and "loosed from our infirmity," can we really know what it is to exclaim: "O, the glorious liberty of the children of God!" Are there not many of us who have tried to raise that shout, and have felt like the fettered slave, to whom freedom is but a name? But the liberty triumphantly proclaimed in these words, may be to us a living reality, and Christ has said: "If the Son shall make you free, ye shall be free, indeed."—St. John 8:36.

He of Whom it is written, "Himself took our infirmities, and bare our sicknesses," has made us free from spiritual and physical sickness if we will but accept that healing.

Would anyone say that that does not mean our infirmities, and our sicknesses, just as much as the infirmities of those people whom Christ healed, when He was on the earth? Did He suffer agony and death any more for them than for us? Hundreds and thousands of years can make no difference in Him, Who is the "same yesterday, to-day, and forever," and all the benefits of His loving kindness and tender mercy may be ours to-day.

CHAPTER V
ANOINTING AND
CONSECRATION

WE complain that our faith is weak, and that our prayers are lifeless, but it is no wonder that we cannot expect answers to our prayers, when we have no idea of fulfilling God's conditions. Can you conceive what the glorious result would be, if each one of us, from this moment, strove to obey every command of our King?

O, we are satisfied with such a heedless, half-hearted obedience, such as we would not render even an earthly parent; then we murmur and are inclined to think secretly that we have been faithful, and God has not!

We think if we partly fulfill God's commands, that we have done our duty. Most of us are willing, probably, to pray for our restoration to health, as far as that is concerned, and some of us are willing to call for the ministers or " elders of the church" (the word "elder" was originally presbyter, from which our word priest is a corruption) to pray with us, but the instructions given in regard to anointing the sick person with oil, we consider quite superfluous and do not think of heeding them.

Just here we must bear in mind, that it is not for us to mark out our path of duty, but to follow that which the Lord has marked out for us; and since He enjoins the use of the oil, we may be sure that He has a wise purpose in so doing. How glad we are to heed the slightest wish of a dear earthly friend, whether or not we deem it of importance, and how much more ought we to feel thus toward our Heavenly Father, whose will, in its minutest details, is always important.

Some may believe that the anointing spoken of in connection with healing the sick, was merely in conformance with some unimportant Jewish custom, but its significance, if we inquire into it, will be found deep and peculiarly sacred. It is not simply anointing the sick person with oil, but "anointing him with oil in the name of the Lord." Profane, indeed, would that man be, who dared perform an idle or meaningless ceremony, in the name of the Lord of Hosts; and if we search the Scriptures for light on this subject of sacred anointing, we shall attach a deeper meaning to the command in James than ever before.

Turning to the book of Leviticus, and reading the laws, "which were a shadow of good things to come," we find that oil was greatly used for sacred purposes, especially for anointing the priests and for offering it with the sacrifices.

"And when any will offer a meat offering unto the Lord, his offering shall be of fine flour, and he shall pour oil upon it, and put frankincense thereon." This is only one of the many texts which refer to the mingling of oil with the sacrifices.

Commenting upon the frequent use of oil in olden times, a learned bishop writes: "Oil was anciently in very high esteem among the eastern nations on various accounts, and as they were wont to express almost every matter of importance by actions as well as words, one way of setting anything apart and appropriating it to an honorable use, was by anointing it with oil. Therefore we find Jotham, in his parable, makes the olive tree speak of its fatness as that 'wherewith they honor God and mati.' — Judges 9:9. Accordingly the tabernacle and temple and their furniture were consecrated by anointing them. And almost every sacrifice had oil mixed with flour added to it when it was offered up."

Both the sacrifices and the priests were, of course, typical of Christ's atonement and Priesthood, and the significance of the typical anointing is made clear to us in passages like the following: St. Peter says: "That word, I say, ye know how God anointed Jesus of Nazareth with the Holy Ghost and with power. Who went about doing good and healing all that were oppressed of the devil, for God was with Him." The wonderful and blessed anointing of the Holy Spirit, first poured upon Jesus Christ, and then through His mediatorial office, shed forth on His faithful followers, was the precious fulfilling of the Levitical foreshadowing.

We read in the prophecy of Isaiah: "And it shall come to pass, in that day, that his burden shall be taken away from off thy shoulder, and his yoke from off thy neck, and the yoke shall be destroyed, because of the anointing."

Deliverance was to come, because of this anointing of the Holy One, and Christ himself, quoting from this same prophet^ says: "The spirit of the Lord is upon me, because He hath anointed me to preach the gospel to the poor, He hath sent me to heal the brokenhearted, to preach deliverance to the captives and recovering of sight to the blind, to set at liberty them that are bruised." — St. Luke 4:18.

Since Christ's righteousness may be ours, so this anointing of the Holy Spirit may be ours, by faith in Him; as we read: "Now He which establish us with you in Christ, and hath anointed us is God." And again: " But the anointing which ye have received of Him, abideth in you, and ye need not that any man teach you; but as the same anointing teach you of all things, and is truth and is no lie, and even as it hath taught you, ye shall abide in Him."

And this brings us to the precious significance of the anointing of the sick with oil, when prayer is offered for their recovery; it is the outward sign of the inward anointing which is to heal and renew the soul and body. It is the setting apart to a holy use of the new life and strength imparted by the Holy Spirit. As in those olden times the tabernacle and the temple and their furniture were consecrated by anointing them with oil, so we may consider that the " earthly house of this tabernacle" which is the temple of the Holy Spirit, is likewise consecrated as "holy unto the Lord."

While the one important and essential anointing is that of the Holy Ghost, it is also important and very comforting, to obey God's command concerning the anointing with oil.

We read that the disciples, when they were preaching the gospel of repentance, "anointed with oil many that were sick, and healed them."

Dr. Cullis, of Boston, fulfills the literal command and

anoints the forehead of the sick person with oil, when he can be present with the one for whom he is praying. Mr. and Mrs. Mix, Rev. Mr. Allen and Mr. Zeller, all of whom have been very successful in pleading for the restoration of the sick, also anoint with oil in the name of the Lord. Then, if the renewing of the Holy Spirit is to be thoroughly accomplished, we must definitely and solemnly consecrate every power of soul and body to the Lord, and it is indeed a glorious privilege to belong so entirely to Him, that there will be no hindrance to His using us in His blessed service.

What indescribable joy it is, to be used in this way, none can know until they have received God's anointing for the work; but if we are wholly consecrated, nothing can hinder the anointing of the Spirit, for He will seal us with the "earnest of our inheritance."

> "Oh, what a life is theirs who live in Christ;
>   How vast the mystery,—
>
> Reaching in height to Heaven, and in its depth,
>   The unfathomed sea."

When Aaron and his sons were ordained to the priesthood, God instructed Moses to "anoint them and consecrate them and sanctify them," that they might minister unto Him (Ex. 28:41), and we shall find that sanctification may be made ours, as well as the anointing and consecration.

Following the footsteps of our blessed Master, we are to present ourselves "a living sacrifice;" and St. Peter says, "Ye, also, as lively stones, are built up a spiritual house, a holy priesthood, to offer up spiritual sacrifices, acceptable to God by Jesus Christ."

After once making an entire consecration of our souls and bodies, there is one truth to be borne in mind, which, though a solemn one, is full of the sweetest comfort. We are henceforth and forever the Lord's, and under no pretext, whatever, shall we have a right to take back the gift which we have voluntarily laid upon the Altar.

Satan will try to persuade us that the Lord has not accepted us, or that we have not really given ourselves, but we must give all such dangerous suggestions to our Lord, and ask Him to conquer them for us.

"Every devoted thing is most holy unto the Lord he shall not search whether it be good or bad, neither shall he change it." — Lev. 27:33. We need not search our hearts to see whether they are worthy or unworthy of God's acceptance, for only through our Saviour are we " justified by faith," and only by His Spirit can we be made holy.

Once presented unto Him we are his forever, and " the Altar sanctifieth the gift."

"The Lord, the everlasting God,
Is our defense and Rock;

The saving health, the saving strength,
Of His anointed flock."

CHAPTER VI
THE USE OF MEDICINE

A DEAR friend who is beginning to recognize her precious privilege of trusting the Lord for all her needs, wrote me not long ago: "It is a great thing to trust God for everything, and still I am growing more and more to feel that not to trust Him is presumption." In this light it must appear to every fully consecrated child of God, who has learned by faith, His blessed will for us.

But how different are the opinions of those who are not yet acquainted with their Lord's sweet will, and who think it is almost presumption to claim His promises, especially this promised healing of the body. They feel and say that they would not dare ask to be healed in answer to prayer, because they must be submissive and bear their sickness patiently.

Still these same persons would doubtless have no scruples in seeking for remedies with which to prolong life or even effect a cure, and if raised from their beds of sickness, would have no question about its having been best for them to recover. Doubtless, all of us have been as inconsistent as this at some time in our lives, even if we have since been shown our errors, and brought beyond such a narrow range of vision. If we have not thought it wrong to seek for medicines to deliver us from the bondage of sickness, why should we fear to be cured by the "prayer of faith," that more perfect healing institution made ours by Christ's atonement?

But some will ask, "How do I know that it is not my time to die?" To these I would say, would you fear to take medicine lest it might be your time to die? You would not be afraid of the medicine's curing you, if God willed you to die, neither need you fear that you will not die at the right time if you obey God's instructions and have the "prayer of faith" offered for you. With the prayer, the anointing, and the consecration, would come upon your soul greater power of the Spirit than you had ever known before, and He would reveal to you if God's will concerning your body was any different from that in His revealed word. "Likewise the Spirit also helpeth our infirmities; for we know not what we should pray for as we ought; but the Spirit itself maketh intercession for us with groanings which cannot be uttered. And He that searcheth the hearts knoweth what is the mind of the Spirit, because He maketh intercession for the saints according to the will of God" Our duty is to obey God's commands, and then trustfully leave the result with Him.

We most of us know, from a sad experience, that medicine has been as inadequate to meet the needs of our suffering bodies, as the moral law has been insufficient to heal and cleanse our souls. Medicine is a most imperfect institution, as all remedial influences outside of Christ, are, of necessity, imperfect, because belonging to this sin-stricken world. "Every good gift and every perfect gift is from above, and cometh down from the Father of lights, with whom is no variableness, neither shadow of turning."

Under the new dispensation, Christ, the "Great Physician of the soul, has promised to be the Physician of the body also, upon the same condition, that of faith. As there is a vast difference between the child of God and the unbeliever, so I cannot but think that our loving Father would have all of us who have consecrated ourselves as "holy unto the Lord," find our physical, as well as spiritual, healing by faith in Christ. The lessons by which we are withdrawn further and further from the world, and from dependence on human help, teach us to rely more on our Saviour; and is it not a Very precious thought, that by the direct influence of the Holy Spirit, we may be healed, renewed and energized in body as in soul?

We are to be a separate and peculiar people, "a holy people unto the Lord," and as God instituted for Israel of old, laws and privileges which other nations did not enjoy, so it is with His consecrated children now. Whenever the children of Israel despised, and failed to avail themselves of their peculiar privileges, they were brought into affliction. Let us examine ourselves, lest we, through unbelief, reject our special blessings, and so grieve our Heavenly Father.

"There is life for a look at the crucified One."

We have only to look at Him to have the bite of the fiery serpent healed, whether the effect of its venom sin, is in our hearts, or on our bodies.

But as little as medicine has been able to benefit us, it is strange how some of us cling to it, unwilling to give it up even after the "prayer of faith" has been offered for us. While it may not be a sin of itself to use medicine when we are looking to the Lord for healing, it often encourages the sin of unbelief, and is, in most cases, a decided hindrance to the complete cure which our Physician would perform, were we willing to trust Him fully.

Holding on to the medicine certainly implies a lack of faith, and by a careful and truthful examination of the motives which lead any one to use it, after prayer has been offered, we shall see that most of them proceed from the sin of unbelief. Are there not many who are dimly conscious of a feeling that if they gave up the medicine, the Lord might fail to keep His promise? It is indeed a sad thing if we are afraid that He, Who notes each tiny sparrow, will fail to take note of us!

Do they not, in their unbelief, desire to use at least some simple medicine, that they may not be very much worse off if God's word should fail? If Jehovah's faithfulness could fail, in whom can we trust?

We are all apt to invent names and excuses for our unbelief, but if we delude ourselves, we cannot deceive God. We must overcome these subtle temptations by declaring that our Strong Helper cannot fail, and that, if He does, we are ready to let all else fail with Him! Satan flees before a conquering trust like that.

In 2 Chron. 16:12, we read: "And Asa in the thirty and ninth year of his reign was diseased in his feet, until his disease was exceeding great: yet in his disease he sought not to the Lord, but to the physicians. And Asa slept with his fathers." This is a remarkable passage, and shows that the Lord makes a great distinction between our trusting in Himself, and in man whom He has created.

There is danger in putting too much confidence in our fellow-beings, for by so doing we look away from God, and forget to rely on Him. With sad ignorance and foolishness, we attribute to earthly helpers much of the power which belongs alone to our Creator, and especially do we see this true when we notice the homage paid to skill in the medical profession. I believe that some of our most painful lessons are necessary, because we stubbornly refuse to recognize God's overruling providence in our daily lives.

"Thus saith the Lord, Cursed be the man that trusteth in man and maketh flesh his arm, and whose heart departeth from the Lord." — Jer. 17:5.

But what could be more comforting and assuring than the passages following: "Blessed is the man that trusteth in the Lord and whose hope the Lord is. For he shall be as a tree planted by the waters and that spreadeth out her roots by the river, and shall not see when heat cometh, but her leaf shall be green, and shall not be careful in the year of drought, neither shall cease from yielding fruit." — Jer. 17:7, 8. Do you think it could be possible for us to trust in the Lord too much? Trusting in Him, all our needs shall be supplied from an inexhaustible source, even the "fountain of living waters." Others fail because they trust only to natural resources, but if we trust in the one Source of all resources, we " shall not be careful in the year of drought, neither shall cease from yielding fruit." "My God shall supply all your need, according to His riches in glory, by Christ Jesus."

As I was reading the seventh chapter of Judges, I noticed a marked lesson conveyed in the second verse: "And the Lord said unto Gideon, The people that are with thee are too many for Me to give the Midianites into their hands, lest Israel vaunt themselves against Me, saying, mine own hand hath saved me."

The folly and pride of human nature is still in danger of vaunting itself against God and we often forget to say with sincere hearts, "Thine is the kingdom, the power and the glory." Our Lord would have us depend so entirely on Himself, that all who witness His mighty works, cannot fail of ascribing our deliverance to Him, Who alone is able to fight our battles for us.

When we give up all else, and look only to His power, our Physician can cure us speedily because we do not hinder His work by dependence on the "wisdom of this world," which is "foolishness with God." — 1 Cor. 3:19.

The Lord refused to give Israel the victory over the Midianites until He had deprived them of occasion to glory, except in the power of the Lord. "There returned of the people twenty and two thousand, and there remained ten thousand," and, even then, "the Lord said unto Gideon, The people are yet too many."

Of those ten thousand remaining, only three hundred were chosen, into whose hands the Lord would deliver the Midianites.

And so we who are trusting to God to gain for us a victory, which we are assured. from repeated failures, no human power could gain for us, shall find that He will not conquer our enemies for us, until we have relinquished our hold on every earthly prop, which might cause us to "vaunt" ourselves against the Lord.

Those who have become so accustomed to taking medicine, and especially to the use of opiates, that it seems impossible, humanly speaking, to live without them, and who are sighing under the bondage, will read the following accounts of healing in this chapter, with renewed hopes of deliverance.

NORWICH, CONN., November 23rd, 1879. DEAR CHRISTIAN FRIENDS:

I want to tell you what the Lord has done for my household. For over twenty years | my wife was addicted to the use of laudanum, that had been prescribed by a physician, and she thought she could not do without it. I taxed my own ingenuity, to its utmost extent, to contrive how the habit might be broken; but all to no avail. The doctors tried subtitles with the same result. In 1873, in the month of July, I went to a camp-meeting at Sea Cliff, L. I.

On Tuesday, the president of the meeting, Rev. J. S. Inskip,

said: "This morning we will have a faith meeting." A large
number spoke of special answers to prayer; the president
then said: "Now, we want to see if this God, Whom we worship here to-day, does answer prayer. All of you who have petitions you would like to have granted, write them, and sign
your names and places of residence, and send them up to
the stand. We will read them, withholding the name. We will
base these petitions on the promises that have been read."

I, with some four hundred others, sent up our petitions.
I wrote: "For a wife who is addicted to the use of opiates;
that the habit may be broken, and she soundly converted." I
sent the petition to the stand, pledging myself to pray every
day of my life for these petitions. The next February my wife
was taken sick. She had been using opiates a great deal. We
called our family doctor and he prescribed for her. On this
day, as we came out of the room where she was ill, the bottle
of laudanum was on the table by the door. The doctor took
the bottle in his hand and brought it out, saying, "I hope to
God she will never ask for that again."

And she never has, nor has she ever seen it, to my knowledge, for I have it locked up. The doctors say they cannot account for it, and I do not attempt to, otherwise than as God
has answered prayer.

I am very truly yours in faith,
TITUS CARRIER.
HINSDALE, MASS., July 4th, 1880.

Miss JUDD:
You wished me to make a statement of my long "Unset,
and of my wonderful cure. I was taken sick in 1875. I had
not been well all winter, but kept around the house until
March, when a doctor was called. Two days after he came
to see me I was unable to sit up any, on account of the pain
in my back. I had used a number of blisters which gave me
some relief. I grew worse, and three weeks after the doctor
was first called, he wished to consult with another physician.
The disease was pronounced inflammation of the kidneys.
All kinds of medicine were tried. I soon got so I could keep

nothing on my stomach, and would have spells of vomiting, every few moments, for days. All I could take was ice. My head pained me fearfully; was obliged to keep a bag of ice on it day and night. Leeches were tried on my head and they gave some relief. Doctors from other towns were called; they all said our physician was doing all that could be done. I was in such pain, and could take no medicine in my stomach, so the doctor began to inject morphine into my veins. I seemed to gain some then; still my back was very bad and I could not sit up any. The doctor carried me from one bed to another. I had used over fifty blisters. Some of the time I would be more comfortable, and the doctor would think I would be able to sit up a little. A reclining chair was bought and he put me in it a few times, but it made me worse.

Mr. and Mrs. Mix came to see me the twenty-sixth of November, 1879. I was then very helpless, could eat but very little, was using morphine all the time. After prayer for my healing I was enabled to rise up in bed, and, with a little assistance from Mrs. Mix, walked a few feet to a chair; in about half an hour I walked back to the bed alone. I had been in the habit of having morphine injected five or six times in twenty-four hours, and the doctor said it would kill me to leave it off. But in answer to the "prayer of faith" I was enabled to do without it entirely. I am quite strong, now; can walk half a mile to church and back. I feel that I cannot thank the Lord enough for what He has done for me. Yours in faith,

MARY E. MACK,

CHAPTER VII
BELIEVING GOD'S WORD

WHEN we have fulfilled, as far as possible, the command given in the fourteenth verse of the fifth chapter of James, we must believe that, according to the Lord's promise, our disease is rebuked, and we are being made whole.

The great point to remember just here is that God's word is true and we must believe it in spite of every apparent contradiction. These contradictions, if they occur, can be only seeming ones, for God is always faithful; but the devil, who is the father of lies, often deceives us into believing feelings and circumstances instead of God's word.

We have a lesson about this in Christ's healing of the nobleman's son. When this nobleman "heard that Jesus was come out of Judea into Galilee, he went unto Him and besought Him that He would come down and heal his son, for he was at the point of death. "Then said Jesus unto him, Except ye see signs and wonders ye will not believe."

This is apt to be the case with us. When prayer is offered for our healing we are unwilling to believe, unless we feel some wonderful power, or extraordinary sensation. That such sensations are often experienced in connection with faith-healing we admit, but many times they are not, and we are required to believe God's word before we see "signs and wonders." "There are diversities of operations, but it is the same God which worketh all in all." — 1 Cor. 12:6.

It is for us to believe God's word, without deeming it needful to look to anything else for confirmation of that word. God's word confirms itself.

This nobleman, feeling the urgency of the case, and realizing that his son was near death, immediately renewed his pleading: "Sir, come down here my child die." The faith which dared to press its cause so earnestly and yet so humbly, was rewarded by the answer, " Go thy way; thy son liveth." The father had now simply to believe Christ's word; there was nothing else to which he could cling, for he could not immediately see his son, to remark whether his condition was really bettered or not; no visible means had been employed for his restoration; the father must believe that his son was recovering because Jesus had spoken; and His word was true.

What a lesson is this to us! We must believe that Christ fulfills His promises just as soon as we claim them in His name, even before we can see any earthly circumstances to warrant us in our belief. So many of us have yet to learn, how different is faith from sight.

We read, "And the man believed the word that Jesus had spoken unto him, and he went his way." Would not some of us have doubted the cure, until we met the servant who bore the glad tidings of his recovery? So sad, but true, it is, that we would receive the witness of our fellow-beings, and not that of our Creator.

One great step toward gaining the victory is to believe that we have the blessing for which we pray; not that we shall have it at some indefinite, future time, but that it belongs to us just as soon as we have fulfilled the condition, and asked for it in Jesus' name. Christ said: "What things soever ye desire when ye pray, believe that ye receive them, and ye shall have them." — St. Mark 11:24.

What would be the state of our mind if we believed that the things we asked for were really ours? We should not certainly think it necessary to ask for them over and over again; but we should immediately drop all anxiety about the matter, and be filled with thanksgiving. Our attitude of pleading would be changed to one of sure expectation, and we would wait joyfully for the gift which we knew had already been bestowed upon us. We can vanquish Satan by saying, "What I desire is mine according to God's promise, even if I do not yet see that I have it. I believe God's word, not circumstances, and I shall soon see that the blessing is mine, by having it really in possession."

If an earthly friend told us we might have some object just

for the asking, we should have no doubt that it was ours, even before we had finished making the request. Whether or not it was immediately placed in our hands, we should believe it to be ours, and should make our calculations the same as if it were within our grasp.

If we set out with the idea that we cannot believe God's word is fulfilled in us, unless our feelings immediately confirm it, we shall be "like a wave of the sea, driven with the wind and tossed," and the apostle says, "let not that man think that he shall receive anything of the Lord." — Jas. 1:6, 7.

I was talking to an invalid about this, not long ago, and she saw instantly how Satan had been deceiving her. "I see!" she exclaimed; "I did not wait for my feelings to believe that Jesus saved me from my sins, but I have been waiting for my feelings before I would believe that He answered my prayers, and was curing me of sickness. When people have asked how I was, I would tell them I was no better, and so I have been making God a liar. I thank Him for this light!"

We are not, of course, to say that we feet better, unless we do, but we may state the fact that we are being made whole, on the authority of God's word. His word is sure, and if we determine to rely on that, and that alone, our position is secure, and no wind of adverse circumstance can cause us to waver.

Another wonderful help to this life of faith, is to believe that every petition we offer in Christ's name will be heard and answered. Trust to God's time and God's way of answering, but believe that we already have the answer to the faintest prayer uttered in that dear name. Consider each as an important document, because bearing that name of power, and lay them all, by an act of faith, in God's keeping, with the surety that He will not forget them, if we, with our short memories, do; and He will bring to our mind each prayer, with its fulfillment, at the right time. This is such a blessed way; then we shall have no anxiety about any of our prayers, for we shall know that everyone is regarded and remembered by the Father, because He will not pass by the name of His dearly loved Son.

I remember once making a remark to a dear friend, which,

because it involved something of a compliment to herself, she laughingly refused to credit. Upon my asking, half reproachfully, if she could not trust my word, she gave me an answer which has since taught me a lesson in regard to faith. "Yes," she said, "I do believe you, and whenever you say anything, I will believe every word of it, even if it isn't so!"

Our faith in God must be so steadfast that even if the evidence of all our senses should deny His word, we must consider them as deceiving us, and still continue to uphold His faithfulness. Such faith as that never fails to remove, sooner or later, the mountain of difficulty or doubt. It is too true that we often place such confidence in our poor, weak fellow-creatures, and yet refuse to have faith in God. When we have faith in dear earthly friends, we will believe nothing contrary to their word, even if there are many circumstances against them. Beloved, there is only One whose word never fails; let us repose such trust in Him, and "nothing shall be impossible" unto us.

There is a simple test which, in many cases, we may apply to our conduct, which will speedily convince us whether or not we are really believing that our prayers are answered, and that is, to act out our faith. Whatever we really believe, we are ready to act in accordance with. I have heard, through good authority, of a lady who was obliged for many years to use crutches, because one foot was so disabled that she could not step upon it. One Sunday morning, as she was going slowly and painfully to church, the promises came forcibly to her mind, and she was impressed to pray for the healing of her foot. Immediately the thought came to her, "If I really believe that God has answered my prayer, my foot is well, and I can walk upon it as upon the other." She pressed it firmly to the ground, in spite of the most crushing pain, and tried to walk rapidly along without the aid of her crutches. Paying no regard to the pain, which, for a few moments, was intense, she said constantly, "I am healed, according to God's promise." Before she reached the church, her foot ceased paining her, and she realized that it was as whole as the other.

This principle of faith-healing is shown in the account of

the cleansing of the ten lepers. Think of the faith they were required to exercise in order to obey Christ's command, "Go shew yourselves unto the priests." This, they knew, it would be of no use to do unless they were cleansed before the searching examination of the priests took place, but relying on Christ's power and mercy, they went as He had commanded. Unbelief would have prevented them from even starting until they saw that the cleansing had been accomplished, but they accepted the blessing in faith, acting faith, and it was soon given them in reality. "For it came to pass that as they went they were cleansed."

I will relate an instance which a correspondent of mine wrote me not long ago. She says: "Last Sunday morning I was asked whether I were going to church. Not feeling, as I thought, able, I answered, "No." Then one who is not a Christian, said, "Is it not the Christian's duty to sacrifice his feelings?" I simply said "Yes," and made up my mind to go. I knew I could not in my own strength. As the church is a long distance from our home, I usually went in a buggy with a high back to it, but this time was compelled to ride in one without any back, and the road was very rough. As I went down the front steps I felt so weak that I feared I should have to go back, but I asked the Lord continually to help me. While at church I felt that I was resting; returned home, and felt much better for having gone. I made the effort and left the result with God. All glory be to His name for the strength He gave me!"

Should increased suffering come to us, after prayer has been offered for our healing, we must believe that it is because of the healing power which is making us whole.

It will give us comfort to consider the experience of the lunatic whom Christ healed. Immediately after Jesus commanded the devil to come out of the child, we read that "the spirit cried and rent him sore, and came out of him, and he was as One dead, insomuch that many said, he is dead.'

This shows, that in some cases, the healing in answer to prayer may not be apparent at once. The spirit of disease may, in its exit from our tormented bodies, "rend us sore," and prostrate us more than ever for a time. But shall this make us believe for a moment that God is failing to keep His word? as if that word which upholds the universe could fail! Let us be ready even to rejoice if increased pain and weakness are ours after prayer has been offered, feeling sure that it is the departing struggle of the disease which Jesus has rebuked.

There is one point which it is necessary to have positively settled when we first seek our Great Physician for healing, and that is how long we intend to trust Him. If we go experimentally, thinking to confide ourselves to His care for a limited time, or until we see whether or not we receive the desired blessing, we are encouraging unbelief, and placing ourselves in a position to receive constant assaults from the enemy. But if we give our souls and bodies into Christ's loving keeping, and decide once for all to leave them there; if we determine that by His grace nothing shall shake our confidence in Him, who is our Strong Tower, then our faith will be steady and victorious.

We shall then have no anxiety as to the result, for knowing that our all-wise Physician cannot make mistakes, our conquering belief in Him will justify all His providences, however mysterious, Satan may, at times, make them appear to us. We must be willing to stake our own reputation for truth, upon God's faithfulness, even willing to be found a liar to prove His truth. "Yea, let God be true and every man a liar, as it is written, That Thou might be justified in Thy sayings, and might overcome when Thou art judged." — Romans 3:3 But, oh, remember! that no one ever trusted in Him and was confounded.

The Lord says, "They shall not be ashamed that wait for me." — Isaiah 49:23.

> "Faith's beacon light,
> Like star at night,
> Pours forth its Heavenly rays;
> Bids darkness flee,
> Illumes life's sea,
> And justifies God's ways."

CHAPTER VIII
GLORIFYING GOD

WE must beware lest we lose the blessing after it is once ours, by fearing to proclaim the victory until the battle is more fully won. "I will wait and see if it is really going to last, before I tell others what God has done for me," says unbelief, and because some of us yield to this temptation of Satan, we lose what we have gained.

Meet the tempter with the unanswerable truth that God cannot fail, and what He has begun He will finish. We say, perhaps, that we know God cannot fail, but our faith might. Resolve that by His grace it must not, it shall not fail. We shall be strengthening our faith, and getting beyond the possibility of a defeat, if we proclaim God's power and mercy, and the mighty works we are trusting Him to accomplish.

If we allow our unbelief to prevent God's gracious work from going on after we have called Him as our Physician, we are dishonoring His holy name; we are not merely letting go of the blessing we desire, but we are giving occasion to the Lord's enemies to say that He is not able to perform that which He has promised. We should remember about certain people we read of in the Bible, who were so unbelieving, that Jesus could do no mighty work among them. We must desire, above all else, that God shall be glorified in us, and that His faithfulness shall be declared to all the world.

A friend wrote me in a recent letter: "I know, many times, unbelief, or failing to acknowledge blessings already received (for instance, encouragement in prayer, or partial alleviation of pain or distress), often hinders our receiving the great blessings the Lord has for us. If we only have perfect obedience, and perfect faith, or confidence, there is no failure. We must trust our blessed Saviour fully."

Doubt is fatal to faith. Jesus says, "Whosoever shall not

doubt in his heart, but shall believe that those things which he saith, shall come to pass, he shall have whatsoever he saith" And again, "Verily, I say unto you, if ye have faith and doubt not, ye shall not only do this which is done to the fig tree, all things whatsoever ye ask in prayer, believing, ye shall receive."

When we have made every effort to believe, and have acted out our faith as far as possible, it is sometimes the dear Lord's will not to give us, at once, the blessings which we know we have claimed by faith. But we must not let anything make us doubt, for any waiting on His part, to give us according to our faith, is productive of the highest good. He alone knows how precious is the trial of our faith, "being much more precious than of gold that perisheth." But notice, it is not the trying of our unbelief, but the trying of our faith which "worketh patience," and if our faith dissolves itself in doubts, there will be no precious metal to shine the clearer from the fire.

Let me say one word about Satan's deceptions in regard to doubting We must remember that temptations to doubt are not sin unless we yield to them; but if we do not turn instantly from the enemy's first suggestion to doubt, it is almost as fatal as giving up to him at once. The most he wants is that we shall argue with him, and then, of course, he will drag us into mires and quicksands. We must remain on the solid Rock. God will conquer all temptations if we take them at once to Him, and confess how powerless we are, of ourselves, to subdue the enemy. "With us is the Lord our God to help us and to fight our battles."

Even if we feel that we are "beginning to sink," as did Peter, we have only to utter one cry for help, and our Lord is at our side. Peter's prayer was very short; only the words, "Lord, save me!" but help was near him, and it is always near to us, if we will ask for it. "And immediately Jesus stretched forth His hand, and caught him and said unto him, O, thou of little faith, wherefore didst thou doubt?"

In that strong, sure upholding, well might Peter's faith revive; and oh, thank the Lord! He is just as ready to hold each one of us to-day. "Thou hast a mighty arm: strong is Thy hand, and high is Thy right hand."

> "I am so weak, dear Lord, I cannot stand
> One moment without Thee;
> But oh, the tenderness of Thine enfolding!
> And oh, the faithfulness of Thine upholding!
> And oh, the strength of Thy right hand—
> That strength is enough for me."

In close connection with doubt, there is ingratitude to guard against There was only one of the ten lepers that Jesus healed, who turned back to glorify God, "and he was a Samaritan." This last fact is particularly recorded, because the people of Samaria were considered opposers of the true religion.- As a learned commentator expresses it, "In the eyes of a Jew, the imputation of being a Samaritan was the most reproachful possible. The term included everything that was odious and despicable." That this "stranger," as Jesus, with mildness and benignity, termed him, should turn back to worship his Saviour, and render thanks for the great blessing just received, while his companions, who were probably veritable descendants of Israel, went heedlessly on their way, is indeed a matter of remark.

If our conduct is similar to that of the ungrateful nine, is it not because our affections are centered more on some earthly blessing than on the Divine Giver, and in our delight over some earthly gift, we set at naught- the one "Pearl of great price"? And when professing Christians are remiss in what should be their most pleasurable of duties, that of glorifying God "with a loud voice," so that those outside of the fold may hear of His mercies, God will often raise up those who have been "strangers" to the true Israel, to sound praises to His faithfulness.

A truly consecrated heart will desire God's glory above everything else, and will rejoice in its Saviour far more than in any of His gifts, precious as they may be.

> "For if thou not to Him aspire,
> But to His gifts alone,

Not love, but covetous desire,
Has brought thee to His throne.
While such thy prayer, it climbs above
In vain,—the golden key
Of God's rich treasure house of love
Thine own will never be."

When the cleansed leper returned to give glory to Jesus, he received a second blessing, which his companions had forfeited by their ingratitude. "And He said unto him, Arise, go thy way: thy faith hath made thee whole." He had recognized Jesus as his Redeemer, and his faith in Him had made him whole in soul as well as in body.

God grant, my dear friends, that we shall not refuse to give glory to God's name-, but that we may return to Him at once with joyful praises, and realize that we are healed, spiritually as well as physically, when we hear His sweet, assuring voice, " Arise, go thy way: thy faith hath made thee whole." And will not our way then, on which He bids us go, be a clear way and a blessed way? He will make every step of it plain to us, and we shall travel it with rejoicing, for the Lord "preserveth the way of His saints."

CHAPTER IX
VICTORY THROUGH CHRIST

IN this chapter is given the experience of a dear sister, who has been brought triumphantly through the conflict, by the conquering might of her Lord; and before my dear readers listen to the recital of her long illness and wonderful deliverance, I believe that they will be interested in a sweet little poem, which she composed when she had no thought of being freed from her suffering, except by death. To all those who are still helpless, these little verses will be a song attuned to their own heart-longings.

LOST, THE SOUND OF FOOTSTEPS
BY ALICE M. BALL

Lost, the sound of footsteps—my own footsteps; just once more
Do I long to hear the music of my feet upon the floor;
Dream I of the days, now vanished, when my lips first
  learned to talk,
Of the mother's love that fondly taught a little child to walk:
In the silence that surrounds me, tired of silence, tired of pain,
Do I long for hands to guide me, till I've learned to walk again.
Lost, the sound of footsteps; how the days have come and gone,
And my steps, forever silenced, wake no echo in our home.
Music floats about me, sweetly wafted on the air,
And the hum of merry voices sounds about me everywhere,
While I fondly long for music, that can be mine nevermore—
Just the music of my footsteps—my own footsteps on the floor.
Lost, the sound of footsteps; and I wait, day after day,
In the midst of this long silence, where the Master bids
  me stay,
And dream of spacious meadows, where my child feet
  used to roam;
Of the foot-prints left so often on the graveled walks at home.

Does the Father know how restless our weak human feet
  may grow,
And does He guide them just as safely, when they lie in
  shadows so?
Lost, the sound of footsteps; when the soul's work here is done,
When the gates of Heaven are opened, and our Father
  bids me come
From this silence so unbroken by the tread of human feet,
Over where immortal footsteps echo on the golden street,
Then, till then, dear Father, teach me, that through all
  these fearful depths,
In the silence that surrounds me, Thou art guiding still
  my steps;
And when life for me is over, even in Heaven, may I once more
Hear again the sound of footsteps, my own footsteps on
  the floor?

PITTSFIELD, MASS., VALLEY FARM, June 22nd, 1880.
MY DEAR CARRIE:
I consider it a privilege to give, what you have asked, the
story of my release from bondage in answer to the "prayer of
faith"; bondage that was dark, deep and mysterious, and of
eighteen years duration. Two months previous to my twelfth
birthday, I was taken sick at school, with what shortly proved
to be an attack of measles. I was not dangerously ill, and as
soon as could be expected, I was about the house, apparently my former healthy, happy self. But the first ride I attempt-
ed after the illness, brought on a sort of nervous spasm, of
short duration, but sufficiently different from anything I had
ever experienced before, to prove that all was not well. For
six months I was able to take long walks, eat and sleep well,
but steadily creeping upon me I felt those strange inexplica-
ble nervous feelings, that changed life, and my desires concerning it. During the following two years I had severe sick
spells, from which I would rally, after a while, with strong
holds upon hope, but, at length, so thoroughly had disease
overpowered me, I was obliged to succumb, and awful suffering and depression it was my lot to bear. Shortly after my

removal here, began a contest between sickness and health, life and death, which it is neither pleasant, nor profitable, to attempt to describe.

What I have suffered, hoped, and feared, it is beyond my power to tell. Many physicians have attended my case, but although, in some instances, temporary relief has been obtained, nothing permanent has been granted, except the knowledge that, in my case, "vain is the help of man."

After the summer of 1867 I was confined wholly to the house, and mostly to my bed, being, very frequently, for days at a time, utterly unable to lift my head from the pillow, or be moved the least particle without agony. During the summer of 1868, under the careful treatment of Dr. A. M. Smith, of this city, I was much relieved of spinal and nervous trouble, and shall never cease thanking God for timely aid afforded; for several subsequent years, under this physician's care, had more comfortable times allotted me than I had known for a long period of time before, but a sufferer I was still, and must have remained, had not the dear Master graciously interposed in my behalf.

I was unable to walk or stand one moment alone upon my feet, a terrible dizziness, and pressure in the heart, attending every attempt of this kind. The cords of my lower limbs were contracted. For sixteen years I had not been able to lie an instant upon my left side; could take but small quantities of food, and often, for weeks at a time, was unable to take the least nourishment without great increase of pain. In one of your letters you speak of what you suffered from "exaltation of sensibility." How much that means to me! During seasons of great prostration I have lain, for hours at a time, in that condition that had a person entered my room, had there been any unusual noise (how I used to pray that nothing of the kind might occur), I do not know how I could have endured it. My dear mother used to sit in the room adjoining mine, doing all in her power to hinder increase of excitement. I have endured the most excruciating pain, and have suffered about as much, it seems to me, as poor humanity could endure.

How zealously I strove to overcome disease, and regain my health, willing to submit to the most severe experiments suggested by physicians, if offered thereby any hope of relief, many can testify.

Last July, and once more in September, prayer was offered for me by Dr. Charles Cullis, of Boston, Mass. I was blessed spiritually, but was not yet prepared to take hold upon the promises, and claim a physical cure. About this time I was led to plead for a consecrated heart, and began to taste the blessedness of giving myself wholly away to God; began to ask, and receive, answers to my prayers in so remarkable a manner, that I could doubt no longer the willingness of Jehovah to speak to the children of men.

At some future time, I want to give you the particulars concerning special answers to prayer in a time of great wonderment and depression in regard to financial embarrassments.

Very soon reports were brought me concerning the great faith of some colored people of Wolcottville, Conn., (your own case, my dear Carrie, being prominent among those that helped increase my courage), and as these good people were soon expecting to visit Pittsfield, I was advised to see them. But alas! like Naaman, I questioned whether the waters of Israel were any better than those of Pharphar and Abana; why my own prayers, or those of my Christian neighbors, might not avail as much as the prayers of Mrs. Mix. I think one of the most important truths which I have been called to learn, since coming to this life of faith, is, that of all His children the Lord demands obedience.

Looking unto Him, prayerfully, I was led to Mrs. Mix. On the second of November she came to me, prayed with me—friends in various parts of the house uniting in prayer for me at the same time—and without assistance from any human agency, arose and walked no dizziness seized me, nor was there any inclination to fall. I had said in the morning that if, in this life, I was ever able to walk to mother's kitchen and, coming through certain rooms, back to my bed, I would say I was healed.

Before dark, on that long to be remembered Sunday, I accomplished this feat easily, and mother and daughter praised God from fervent hearts. Cords so long contracted straightened in one night. I could now take food regularly without distress, and the word of the Master came to me with power: "Wait on the Lord: be of good courage, and He shall strengthen thine heart; wait, I say, on the Lord." — Psalm 27:14.

I had yet to learn many lessons, however; among other things, that what I had now commenced is termed, and is, in very truth, the "fight of faith." I think I have met every foe that Pilgrim encountered on the first part of his journey from the city of Destruction, from Worldly Wiseman down to Simple and Presumption; each has had his say. Thanks be to God, 1 am trusting still.

Not many days had passed before old symptoms returned, and, according to human appearances, there was need of medicine. The tempter began an argument with my soul, somewhat difficult to resist, telling me that I could go no further without this, which had been my help so many years. In an agony of suspense and fear I came direct to God for light, for direction; and He spoke peace to my soul. I gave orders for my medicine to be thrown away; whether I could lift my head or not, I would trust!

Among other inestimable blessings, my Lord has granted me a mother strong in faith; when my own began to waver, hers but shone the clearer, and together we fought on. On the third of November, walking a short distance from our door, I had plucked a green leaf and borne it triumphantly to mother, by whom it was received as truly an evidence that the waters were abating, as was the olive leaf by Noah. I gained so rapidly, that, in the course of a few weeks, taking a friend's arm and a cane, I walked across the street to sister's.

O, it is all too glorious to describe, the wondrous way my Lord has led me on, seeming sometimes "for a small moment" to have forsaken me, but with "everlasting mercy" bearing me in mind. Gradually (my first word from the dear Lord, when I came to Him for healing, had been "wait") my faith and strength increased, until I could walk some little distance on the frozen earth each day, and make short calls at near neighbors. We had lived in our house for seventeen years, and never, until since my cure, had I seen the upper rooms. Each trip upstairs seemed as new, and grand, and strange, as most people's trips to Europe! Meanwhile, matters had been so arranged that the coming spring, my only sister was expecting to move one mile away, and was very desirous of taking mother and myself with her to her new home; but above everything, this side of death, stood my dread of riding. For eighteen years every attempt to ride had occasioned spasms, followed by such long prostration as was terrible to recall, and just here Satan stood over me exultant for many days.

I did not always wisely remember that God's Word does not promise aid in advance of trial, but "as thy day so shall thy strength be." When the full time for my first experience in the carriage came, the recollection of the agony I had endured in times past, for a moment overpowered me; my strength left me, my heart grew tremulous, and I called mightily unto God for help, for some word of cheer. Opening the good Book, expectantly, I was directed to these words: "He giveth power to the faint, and to them that have no might He increaseth strength." — Isaiah 40:29. What could I ask more?

I went to the carriage, praising God. Victory did not crown my first effort, nor the next, but knowing that my Lord had promised —victory must be mine. All in good time it came; no larger than the cloud for which Elijah waited, was its first appearance, but by degrees I found that I could bear the motion of the carriage, and still better as time went on. I could be drawn slowly across the yard, but the thought of that one-mile drive terminating in change of home and surroundings, which I was so soon expected to undertake, Satan was permitted to hold before my mind's eyes for many days and nights, harassing me with doubts and fears, terrible to endure. On the twentieth of May, in an easy carriage phaeton, drawn by a gentle horse, I rode a quarter of a mile without spasms or any great distress. Victory was mine; friends stood upon the sidewalk, speaking words of encouragement and praise as we passed along, and the thankfulness that went up from my heart that afternoon, no one but the dear Master knows anything about.

Now I began coming to the dear Lord for unwavering faith concerning that long-dreaded removal to my new home, and on the morning of the second of June, little dreaming that that was the day appointed by the dear Master, for the same, my cry unto Him was answered by these words of promise, "Behold I am with thee, and will keep thee in all places whither thou goest for I will not leave thee until I have done that which I have spoken to thee of."—Gen. 28:15.

There had been no time appointed for my transit to other quarters, but that June morning it was as if my Lord had told me that the time was near at hand. To my great amazement, nervous anxiety was removed. I was wonderfully at rest, and began making preparations for a hasty exit; whether That day, or three months from that day, none but the dear Lord knew.

During the early part of the afternoon I was enabled to call at a certain neighbor's, whom I had desired to visit before leaving our old home, and make a farewell call at another place not far away. Returning home, somewhat exhausted, I sought my bed for rest, and rest was granted. And now, at the right moment, my brother-in-law, at his store some little distance away, whom I had not seen for some time, and to whom no one had spoken of calling for me to ride that day, was impressed to come to us with horse and phaeton. The time was now fully come. I was gloriously strengthened; rode to my new home without injury, or any great fatigue. Was not my Lord fulfilling His word of promise, gloriously? Is it any wonder if my soul is so filled with praise that the one hundred and third Psalm will keep surging up from its very depths? I have given you a somewhat lengthy account, but the story can never be half told. I am in a delightful place to praise God all the day long, am growing stronger and better as the days go by, have long since lain on my left side; in short, am being made every whit whole, thanks be to God, Who "giveth us the victory through our Lord Jesus Christ."

ALICE M. BALL.

CHAPTER X
PRAYER AND FASTING

IF the "fight of faith" looks difficult for us. we must not give up the blessings for which we have pleaded, and shelter ourselves behind the thought that it is not God's will for us to have them, when really our unbelief prevents us from obtaining them. The cowardice which makes us flee before the enemy., is not the submission of faith; and we must not mistake the one for the other. There is one instance in which we read of the disciples failing to restore the sick, and that was when they could not cast the evil spirit out of the poor lunatic.

When our Saviour Himself had performed the miracle, "Then came the disciples to Jesus apart, and said, Why could not we cast him out? And Jesus said, Because of your unbelief."

If the disciples had reasoned, as some Christians of this age undoubtedly would, they would have said to the poor father, after their ineffectual attempt to cast the devil out of his child, "You had better go home and bear your affliction patiently. It is not the will of God that your son should be cured." But Jesus tells the disciples, in plain language, the reason of their failure, "Because of your unbelief."

Since He adds immediately after, "Howbeit this kind goeth not out but by prayer and fasting," it would seem to imply that this humiliation and denying of the body, would develop their spirituality, and take away from their own hearts the blind spirit of unbelief. It certainly teaches us that some difficulties which cannot be overcome by prayer alone, can be conquered by prayer and fasting. By subduing our fleshly appetites I believe that we become prepared for a higher spirituality; and with the renewing of the Holy Spirit, our requickened faith is powerful enough to grasp the blessings awaiting us.

Do Christians attach enough importance to this subject of fasting? Our fleshly desires are clamorous, and not easily put aside. Most of us satisfy our consciences, even in seasons of fasting which the Church proclaims, by denying ourselves some luxury, which, in the solemn earnest life of a Christian, ought not to be considered by us allowable at any time. Christ said, " But the days will come when the Bridegroom shall be taken away from them, and then shall they fast in those days." We read many times in the book of Acts, that the disciples did fast after the Heavenly Bridegroom had been taken away, and since He has not yet returned, is it not meet for us also to deny ourselves, at times, the bread for which we hunger again, that we may be satisfied with the Bread of Life? And considering the new spiritual life which may be ours through this means, Christ's question, "Is not the life more than meat?" comes to us with a new interpretation.

Our holy Saviour, Himself, set us the example of fasting, when for " forty days and forty nights" He hungered for our sakes, and He has plainly told us that a reward from the Father shall be given us, when we thus humble ourselves before Him. Speaking Drovingly of the Pharisees who disfigured their faces that they might appear unto men to last, He continues, "But thou when thou fastest, anoint thine head and wash thy face, that thou shall not appear unto men to fast, but unto thy Father which seeth in secret, and thy Father which seeth in secret shall reward thee openly."

Some of us may be faithless enough to believe that it would be impossible to deny ourselves one meal, even, without great weakness of body, and subsequent prostration, but my experience in this has shown me that the higher sustenance given at such a time, is ample nourishment for the body as well as the soul.

One sweet, Christian sister, of my acquaintance, who was praying with fasting for a certain result which she desired for the glory of God, was marvelously sustained. Far from strong, naturally, she went without food long enough to have weakened a much stronger person, but she was nourished by the Lord. She had never before fasted for so long a tin but "ever so comfortably," she told me, and afterwards, to the Lord's praise, she felt as well and strong as usual.

We may remember with comfort how out tender Shepherd said, "I have compassion on the multitude, and I will not send them away fasting, lest they faint in the way." — St. Matt, 15:32. And can we think that He will not also "have compassion " on us when we "continue with" Him in weakness of body, pleading our needs, or the needs of our friends? He will not send us away fasting. He will feed our souls with Himself, the Heavenly Manna. Think how the poor woman of Canaan was rewarded when she had faith even to claim the crumbs which the "children" had let fall.

And here I cannot help speaking of that wondrous means of grace and strength, the Sacrament of the Lord's Supper, of which I fear too many of us fail to avail ourselves. Shall our souls starve while so rich a banquet is awaiting them?

O, dear ones, we are all invited as children to eat at the table of our Lord and Master, but do we have any appreciation of the wondrous feast set before us, even the "Bread of Life " i Even if we do not refuse to partake of this sacred feast, are we making the most of our precious privileges, or are we dropping larger portions than "crumbs " from our heedless and irreverent grasp? Do we "gather up the fragments that remain, that nothing be lost"?—St. John vi: 12. I believe that if we will accept all that He offers us in that holy and mystical body, of which we spiritually partake, we may find renewed physical life as well as spiritual. Even if the lesser benefits are only "fragments" compared with the greater, we must not overlook or despise them.

> "Shepherd of souls, refresh and bless
> Thy chosen pilgrim flock,
> With manna in the wilderness,
> With water from the rock.
>
> "Hungry and thirsty, faint and weak,
> As Thou when here below,
> Our souls the joys celestial seek
> Which from Thy sorrows flow.

"We would not live by bread alone,
But by that word of grace.
In strength of which we travel on
To our abiding-place.

"Be known to us in breaking bread,
But do not then depart;
Saviour abide with us, and spread
Thy table in our heart."

But to continue the subject of prayer and fasting. Why were those thousands of people with Jesus on the occasion of His feeding them with bread in the wilderness? We read, "And great multitudes came unto Him, having with them those that were lame, blind, dumb, maimed, and many others, and cast them at Jesus' feet, and He healed them." The people who were well and strong were bearing their sick friends to Christ, and, for their sakes, they had followed Him, and were without bread in the wilderness. And ought we not thus, with prayer and fasting, to bring the unconverted, the sick and the feeble, and lay them at Jesus' feet?

The third chapter of Acts affords us many lessons in regard to our duty toward our suffering neighbors. The poor lame man lay daily at the " Gate Beautiful," and asked alms of those who entered the temple, just as there are many nowadays, crippled spiritually and physically, watching us with eager eyes as we enter the sacred precincts, only in the shadow of which they may lie; and is it not our faithlessness that prevents us from bidding them, in the name of Christ, "rise up and walk," that they too may enter the "Church Militant" in triumph?

We read that this lame man, at Peter's bidding, "leaping up stood, and walked, and entered with them into the temple, walking and leaping and praising God." What a glorious entrance was that; rejoicing in strength of body and soul, he was ready to serve God with both. But we must look back to notice that Peter did more than to bid him arise and walk; "he took him by the right hand, and lifted him up."

So we must feel it our duty to assist those who are weak in faith, and those who have never had power to stand, and by prayer and encouragement we must hold them up, until they receive strength to "walk and leap." We read further about this converted and healed man, "And all the people saw him walking and praising God and they were filled with wonder and amazement at that which had happened unto him." It is probable that the people were as much amazed at the man's praising God, as at his walking, and just in this glorious way, my dear, Christian friends, do we want to fill the world and the Church "with wonder and amazement " at the conversion of sinners, and the healing of sufferers, and bring into the Church those who have long lain outside in poverty of soul, or weakness of body.

We will glance at the other important lessons in this account of healing. It is related that "all the people ran together unto them in the porch that is called Solomon's, greatly wondering. And when Peter saw it he answered unto the people, Ye men of Israel why marvel ye at this? or why look ye so earnestly on us, as though by our own power or holiness we had made this man to walk?" We find human nature now, as Peter found it then. So many look wonderingly at the instruments of God, believing them possessed of some mysterious power, or else believing them capable, by their own holiness, of obtaining blessings which only the righteousness of Christ can procure for any of us.

Peter proceeds to explain clearly the principle of faith-healing: "The God of Abraham and of Isaac and of Jacob hath glorified His Son Jesus, and His name through faith in His name hath made this man strong whom ye see and know: yea, the faith which is by Him hath given him this perfect soundness in the presence of you all."

O, my dear friends, we are not told that Christ was glorified by the man's forty-years' affliction, but by the "perfect soundness" given him by faith in our Saviour's name. "Therefore, glorify God in your body and in your spirit, which are God's."

The efficacy of prayer and fasting for ourselves and for our suffering friends, was brought very forcibly to my mind by a letter which I received from an acquaintance, a while ago, and which caused me to search the Scriptures, to get more light on our duty in this respect. The letter was from a minister, who had been cured of consumption after his wife had prayed with fasting, when many prayers without this bodily humiliation had failed to secure the desired healing. I have obtained permission of my friend to publish his interesting letter, thinking it may strengthen the faith of some of the dear sufferers who read this book.

ALEXANDER, N. Y., April 16th, 1880.

DEAR SISTER IN CHRIST:

I have had great interest in your case from the time you were taken sick, and when I knew of your being healed I could praise God with you. I have had an experience somewhat like yours, or as wonderful.

After I moved from Linden to Boston, I was taken sick; having taken a severe cold, being very much overworked, but so situated that I could not stop work, and attend to myself, and soon took another cold, and another, until I was compelled to give up and go home, as many thought, to die of quick consumption. I called two skillful physicians, but they both told my friends I must die. I was confined to my house, and my neighbors expected to see crape on the door at any time.

I did not think I was going to die, but believed the Lord was going to raise me up in answer to the "prayer of faith;" but as I was so weak in body, I thought it must be someone's faith beside my own. After looking to the Lord for several days, and getting worse all the time, I wrote a line to Dr. Cullis, and sent my daughter to the "Consumptives' Home " with it, with the request for Dr. Cullis to come and pray for me.

I told my daughter if he was not there to bring the letter back to me, and as he was not there she brought it back. My wife then said, "You have prayed for others, and they have been healed; why can't you pray for yourself?" I was so weak in body, it did not seem as though I could have the faith. I waited a whole week, getting worse and worse, and had fearful night-sweats, and, to all human appearance, I was in the last stages of consumption. Finally my wife was fasting all day, praying the Lord to give me healing-faith, though I knew nothing of it. That very night I called my wife and children to my couch, and asked if they had any faith, and they all replied, "yes."

I then took my Bible, turned with trembling hands, and read several promises on prayer and faith, and also that "the prayer of faith shall save the sick and the Lord shall raise him up," and we prayed and united our faith, claiming the promise, "if two of you shall agree on earth, as touching anything that they shall ask, it shall be done."

As we were praying, I felt a sensation from my head down my spine, and to my feet, like the shock from a battery, and I knew I was healed. In ten days' time I was at my work again in the office of "The Christian," and preached Sundays, and, from that day till this, I have had no trouble with my lungs. O, what a spiritual blessing I received also; it seemed as though I never felt Jesus so near before, not even at my conversion. I was healed Oct. 26th, 1876. I have known of very many cases of faith-healing. My wife has been healed, and is alive now in answer to prayer, though my friends thought she must die. O, what a mighty Saviour we have! Let us praise and exalt him.

Yours in Christ,
(Rev.) A. P. MOORE.

Mr. Moore speaks of his wife's healing, and I have requested her account of it for my readers. Mrs. Moore is known to me personally, and the example of her beautiful Christian life is helpful to all who know her. The following letter was received from her a short time ago:

ALEXANDER, N. Y.
MY DEAR SISTER IN CHRIST:
I have many times been raised up in answer to prayer. Many times when medicine has failed to help, have I and the children been restored when we looked to God alone, and let go wholly of the help of man. O, I have found it blessed to take the Lord for our Physician. Two years ago the doctor said mine was a very doubtful case; I might live but a very short time. My disease was a most dangerous one, and could not be successfully reached by remedies, being internal cancer. I doctored four months with a physician who was very skillful

with such diseases, and was then no better, as I could realize, but seemed much weaker.

I grew worse and worse; tried remedies that had helped others, but they did me no good. My pain grew much more severe. I realized that I was at death's door. My husband then requested prayer for me through a Christian paper, the "Crisis," begging those who had faith to pray for me, saying that he felt like a drowning man, crying for help, and saying who will help ?—who?" Prayer was offered for me, not only by our people, but also by a little band of faithful Pilgrims in E. Bethany, called Free Methodists.

God heard and answered. I was filled with the Holy Spirit. Every part of my body underwent a change, a renovation. My strength came, and I commenced to walk; had hardly stepped at all for several months. O, how thankful I did feel; how I did praise the Lord "with a loud voice." I gave Him glory, and, thanks be to His dear name! I have walked ever since. I can now work very hard nearly all day. The Lord has healed me, and I shall yet praise Him for a complete cure.

I have another case of recent date. A young lady, who was living with one of our neighbors, was troubled with her lungs exceedingly. They were in a serious condition, and she was quite unfitted for work. Providentially, my husband and I staid there one night, shortly after I was healed. I felt impressed to pray for her recovery, and was greatly blessed. Was filled with the Spirit in a great measure, as when I was healed myself. She was healed that very evening. All through the night she felt the healing Power. It was something like a prickling or itching sensation. She has had no trouble with her lungs since, and has worked exceedingly hard a great share of the time. She gave God all the glory, and was greatly blessed spiritually. I have received a greater blessing spiritually, when I have been healed, than even at my conversion.

O, how good the Lord is, to thus condescend to hear our cries for help, and thus to relieve us. May we never grieve Him more by unbelief. God help us to accept all His promises, and be truly blessed. Should you desire more of our experience of the healing power of God, I can give you many instances where we have been healed immediately. When we gave up all medicine, and trusted God wholly, He never disappointed us.

Your sister in faith and hope,

MRS. A. P. MOORE.

"He that trusteth in the Lord, mercy shall compass him about." — Psalm 32:10.

"It is better to trust in the Lord than to put confidence in man. It is better to trust in the Lord than to put confidence in princes." — Psalm 118:8, 9.

"The Lord is my strength and my shield; my heart trusted in Him, and I am helped: therefore my heart greatly rejoiceth; and with my song will I praise Him." — Psalm 28:7.

CHAPTER XI
SERVICE FOR THE MASTER

THERE are two short verses in the eighth chapter of St. Matthew, which we are not apt to consider of particular importance, but which, in reality, contain a very sweet and comforting lesson. "And when Jesus was come into Peter's house, He saw his wife's mother laid and sick of a fever. And He touched her hand, and the fever left her, and she arose and ministered unto them."

When Christ thus bids us arise, we shall find a blessed work in ministering to all who need our ministrations, and however humble may be our work seemingly, it will be sweetened by the precious knowledge that we are doing it for Him. Yes, as much for Him if we offer only a "cup of cold water" in His name, as when this restored woman ministered unto the Lord of Hosts, Himself.

He "rebuked the fever" and raised her from her bed of sickness that she might minister unto her Lord and those of her household. He would not have needed her services had He not chosen to accept them, for it would have been as easy for Him to perform some other miracle as that one, but He knows the joy which a fully restored and consecrated soul finds in loving service, and He gave to her, as He is willing to give to us, the privilege of being useful to Him.

It is very noticeable that all who experience this Divine healing are filled with the desire to be useful in the Master's vineyard. Timid souls who have been either afraid or ashamed to speak for Christ, are ready, after His healing touch, to proclaim to all the beauty of their Saviour. Verily, He giveth sight to the blind, and speech to the dumb.

One dear sister of my acquaintance, who recovered from a long and painful illness, in answer to the "prayer of faith," has since found her greatest joy in winning souls for the

Master. Her efforts in this direction, and especially her labors among the victims of intemperance and vice, have been rejoiced over by many who have found "the Way of Salvation" through her prayerful ministry. Her own experience of her Saviour's restoring grace, and of His healing touch, is well calculated to give renewed courage and faith to others, and I publish entire the account which she has, at my request, kindly written for this work.

BUFFALO, June 10th, 1880.

I have often felt, since my recovery from a long and alarming illness, in answer to the "prayer of faith," that I should make a public statement of the facts of the case, both that God's name might be glorified by a recital of His wonderful dealing with me, and that some suffering ones who feel that there is nothing before them but a life of pain, may, through the blessing of the Holy Spirit, be led, as I have been, to look unto Him, "Who healeth all our diseases." I trust, too, that there may be professing Christians, who have heretofore followed the Master but "afar off" and with weak and faltering faith, who may be quickened into a new life by its perusal. God grant that it may be so, for His dear name's sake!

There are many in this city who will recall the long weary years of my illness. I believe it was partly caused by the worldly life of dissipation, into which I plunged at the age of eighteen, and which I bent every energy to maintain for several years, in spite of growing weakness and steady decline of nervous force, which warned me that the taper was burning low.

O, how bitterly do I regret those wasted years! It was one continual round of parties, operas and theatres throughout the winter season, only to be continued at some fashionable watering place, when summer came. Self was my only thought, and self-gratification my only ambition. Truly, when I reflect upon that period of my life and compare it with the present, I can say, with Paul, "The things I once loved, now I hate, and the things I hated, now I love."

Such a life is worse than useless; it is suicidal, and I cannot too strongly warn my young readers against it. The path appears to be a rosy one, but oh! the thorns lie underneath. At last I was forced to take my bed, and from that time, for a period of ten years, I was an invalid, suffering more in mind and body than any language of mine could describe.

But although, through the skill of an Indiana physician, I was, at the close of a year, enabled to walk about, I had learned so little by my sufferings that I, at once, by a great effort of will, returned to my former life of gaiety and folly, and, after a few months, the Lord in mercy laid His correcting hand upon me, and once more I was confined to my bed.

The nervous system seemed to be completely prostrated; there was a constant pressure, at times intense, in the back of my head, with great spinal irritation, which twice resulted in a serious attack of congestion of the brain, threatening my life. There was nervous dyspepsia in its worst form, attended by difficulties of the bowels and kidneys, which greatly increased my sufferings. There were other painful diseases to which I fell a victim at the beginning of my illness, and which medical aid never reached.

When I look back and consider the deplorable condition I was in, and how much I am able to endure to-day, I can only exclaim, "This is the Lord s doings, and it is marvelous in my eyes."

It is not too much to say that I suffered a living death with my head. Very little of the time was I able to read, or hear reading, or see any of my friends. One of my sisters came from a distant city several times to see me, but I was too ill to bear the excitement of seeing her.

The slightest noise caused my nerves to vibrate with the keenest agony; there could be no sweeping done within my hearing (which was marvelously acute) for many weeks—all sounds being magnified to my sensitive brain. Several friends and relatives sickened and died, and I did not learn of it until years had passed—no one daring to tell me, lest the shock should prove more than I could bear.

Not the least of my distress was the thought that I must die, and that no one would be the better for my having lived; that my life had been utterly selfish and sinful; that I had no treasure laid up in Heaven, and that I was wholly unprepared to enter there.

At last, after having been under the care of seven different physicians, and being advised by the one then attending me, to once more seek a change of air and treatment, I was carried away upon a mattress with little, if any, hope in the minds of my distracted parents, that I could live many weeks.

As for myself, I clung to life simply because I was afraid to die. After having received some benefit from magnetic treatment, and having been absent from home nearly three years, I was able to ride out, and walk about my room, but the relief was only temporary. It was then that, after having had in all nine physicians, the Lord led me to the dear, Christian woman, in the city of Rochester, who pointed me to Jesus, the Great Physician—glory be to His name!—as the remedy I needed for my sin-laden soul, and my suffering body. Oh, that I could find words to express what a revelation that was to me!" Oh, for ten thousand tongues to speak my great Redeemer's praise!" His wondrous love, His almighty power! Dear reader, if you have never tasted that power, nor the faithfulness of His promises toward us who believe, may the Holy Spirit incline your heart to do so now. Like a sudden flood of sunlight in the gloomiest day, His heavenly light shone in upon my darkened soul, and, flinging myself in utter self-abasement at his feet, I cried, "Lord, if Thou wilt, Thou canst make me clean!"

At that time I was, for the first time in my life, "hungering and thirsting after righteousness," and had felt that hungering from the first interview held with this saintly woman, whose very presence filled me with a deep awe and a sense of my great impurity and sinfulness. Many times during the morning Bible reading, at her house, I have trembled so violently from the powerful influence of the Holy Ghost which fell upon us as she spoke, that I could scarcely retain my seat.

Coming thus in true penitence, humility and faith to Jesus, I found Him all that my soul could ever need, and then re-

joicing in the forgiveness of my sins, I was led to look to Him
for healing of the body also. I vowed to Him that if he would,
in mercy, restore me to health, my life should be wholly consecrated to His service. He heard my cry and delivered me
from my distresses. To Him "be glory and majesty, dominion
and power, both now and ever! Amen."

I had been carried up and down-stairs for nearly five years;
in ten days I walked down and out into the street and back
to my room with a little assistance. In a few weeks, not more
than four, I could walk two miles without injury, and a short
time after this was sent home, a wonder and an astonish-
ment to all who knew me. It seemed to be God's plan with me
to greatly try my faith by permitting some of my difficulties
to remain, in spite of many prayers and efforts to overcome,
and also by sending me many afflictions and sorrows, which
well-nigh caused my frail bark to sink beneath the waves.
But with the Captain of our salvation on board I felt that I
should weather all the storms. During those times of fiery
trial, when flesh and heart almost failed me, I was often com-
forted by sweet words of Scripture stealing in upon my mind
so gently; Heavenly promises, re-assuring and urging me on.
From my heart I thank my Heavenly Father for the griefs
and trials He has sent me, for each has brought its deep and
valued lessons, and each has brought me nearer and nearer
to Him. "Before I was afflicted I went astray, but now have I
kept Thy law."

Within the past two years I have been still further strengthened by an interview with a minister of the Gospel, in the
city of Brooklyn, who had been miraculously healed, almost
instantly, while engaged in prayer with Dr. Cullis, of Boston,
whose great work of faith is widely known. He bade me believe that the work of healing was wholly done in me, though
I could not see it so, reminding me that "we walk by faith and
not by sight."

While pondering over this, as I walked the street some days
after, very much mystified as to his meaning, and questioning his authority for saying so, the following verse from God's
Word rushed through my mind with a meaning it had never

before: "What things soever ye desire, when ye pray believe that ye receive them and ye shall have them "! That is, believe though it be in total darkness, and light will surely come. Joshua had to take God's word for it that Jericho was his, and, in obedience to His command, gave the shout of victory before there was the least sign of it, and then the walls fell!

I gladly grasped the above-named promise, feeling assured that the Lord had sent it for my encouragement, and was greatly strengthened thereby, and upon returning home was very soon led out into the Master's vineyard, in a most unexpected way, to labor in a city mission work, a work which I hope never to be compelled to abandon. It brought me into many scenes of the most harrowing description, and surely was a work better calculated to test my nervous strength, than anything I could have possibly found. I could not have endured it without God's sustaining grace; neither could I ever have chosen such a work for myself. It was clearly God's leading, and so I followed on.

Two months ago, feeling much worn by the many perplexities and anxieties, inseparable from such a work, I felt the necessity of calling a little meeting of believing ones, for united prayer that I might be strengthened, and fully equipped to do the work which pressed upon me on all sides, especially all the reading and writing I found necessary day by day, and which had seemed for a time more than my brain could bear.

We also asked that, above all, I might be "endued with power from on high." Six friends united with me in this city at the hour appointed, and Mr. and Mrs. Mix, in Wolcottville, Conn., and I was "anointed with oil in the name of the Lord," according to the command in James 5:14, by an "elder of the church" who was present. All in the room felt the power of the Spirit, and it was an hour long to be remembered. Those prayers were heard and answered! Two days after, I was called very suddenly to scenes of the most trying description, and of the most unexpected nature, where strength of mind and body were fully tested. My friends agree with me that I was led of the Spirit to call the prayer-meeting just when I did, and that I was indeed prepared by the Lord for all the difficult work which immediately followed.

I am well aware how this statement will be received by the incredulous world, and by many earnest followers of the Master to where the subject is a new one; but to the latter 1 would say, take your Bible and prayerfully read the many precious promises given to His believing children. Bear in mind that they are all conditional. It is always "according to thy faith be it unto thee." Just think for one moment what Jesus said to the distracted father who brought to Him his son who was vexed with a devil: "If thou canst believe, all things are possible to him that believeth"! Is not the magnitude of that promise almost overwhelming? Is it not boundless? And does it not mean any man, woman or child who lived then, who lives now, or who may live in the future, who truly believes? Does He not invite and persuade us to test His faithfulness and His almighty power? And we need not fear to bring every little need of soul and body to Him, for He says, "My God shall supply all your need," and "Whatsoever ye shall ask the Father in My name. He will give it you." Our bodily needs are often very imperative, often entirely beyond the reach of human aid. Then why not carry them to Jesus, who has "all power in heaven and on earth "? It is so sweet, so comforting to feel that we have a loving Father Who notes even the tiny sparrow's fall, and Who assures us that we "are of more value than many sparrows."

In giving us His only Son to die the shameful death of the cross, He has proved "the great love wherewith He hath loved us," and that we are indeed precious in His sight. He loves to give good gifts to His children more than the tenderest earthly parent can, and therefore I think we have every encouragement to come and bring all our needs, small and great, before Him, claiming the promise that "no good thing will He withhold from them that walk uprightly."

An unbelieving relative, to whom I related a wonderful instance of immediate relief, in answer to my prayer, from a very painful malady with which I was attacked at one time, since my recovery, said, after critically listening to the recital, "Well, a few facts are worth a great many surmises!" And so

I feel that the large number of facts which have been ascertained within the past fifteen years with regard to the healing of all manner of disease, chronic and acute, in answer to the prayer of faith, are sufficient to convince any candid inquirer who will investigate the subject with a sincere desire to be guided into all truth. It is a lack of knowledge, as well as a sad lack of faith, which makes the Christian Church so slow to receive the testimony of those who have been healed by coming to Jesus as did the suffering ones of old. Our Saviour promises to manifest Himself unto His faithful followers as He would not to the world. Therefore how dare any man say that these things, related in many instances by persons justly eminent for their devoted, holy lives, are not true, simply because he in his darkness and unbelief has not been similarly blest?

It is our privilege to trust Jesus as a perfect Saviour, "able to save, to the uttermost, all who come unto God by Him," and, dear reader, just as willing as He is able. He is able to save us daily and hourly from every known sin, because "Whosoever abideth in Him sinneth not." — 1 John 3:6. He is able to cleanse our hearts from all uncleanness. "The blood of Jesus Christ, His Son, cleanseth us from all sin;" and more than that, He is able to keep our hearts as pure and fit temples for the indwelling of the Holy Ghost. The Bible says, "Without holiness no man shall see God;" and again, "Without faith it is impossible to please God." A life of holiness is attained only by faith, and faith is the gift of God; one of those "best gifts" which St. Paul begs us to "covet earnestly." Every faculty of the mind, as well as every muscle of the body, strengthens by use. Therefore let us exercise what faith we have, and pray for more. The men and women whom I have met who have been led to look to Jesus for restoration to health, are, without exception, leading devout and holy lives, and thus realize the fulfillment of the promises given to all who abide in Christ, and know, as does the writer, the blessedness of being "dead unto sin and alive unto righteousness." Let us surrender ourselves wholly to the Lord. His Word says, " Bring ye all the tithes into the store-house that I may have meat in my house, saith the Lord; and prove me now herewith, if I will not open you the windows of heaven and pour you out a blessing that there shall not be room enough to receive it." Let us accept this challenge, lay ourselves upon the Altar and receive this wondous blessing, and we shall find Him sufficient for every need of soul and body. For myself, I feel to say that God, helping me, "Christ shall be magnified in my body, whether it be by life or by death."

ANNA W. PROSSER.

CHAPTER XII
THE TRUE CHURCH MILITANT

OUTPOURINGS of praise, such as those recorded in the testimonies given in this book, are going up every moment, from increasing multitudes of God's children, who are finding in their loving, tender Shepherd, "an ever present help "in time of all trouble. In their wonderful experience of the richness of His mercy, of the faithfulness of His care, over all their smallest needs, there arise great yearnings that other Christians may understand His boundless love, and praise Him by proving His every promise. O, the blessedness of "casting all our care upon Him," Who careth for us, can never be told. If everyone would obey the command: "Be careful for nothing; but in everything, by prayer and supplication with thanksgiving, let your requests be made known unto God," there would be no troubled hearts or care-worn brows, and only "the peace which passeth all understanding," would shine from faces alight with the joy of the Lord. In the one hundred and seventh Psalm, David enumerates God's full and blessed answers to the prayers of travelers, of captives, of sick persons, of seamen and of husbandmen, and exclaims again and again in wondering adoration, " Oh, that men would praise the Lord for His goodness and for His wonderful works to the children of men!"

And, after summing up God's manifold providences in answer to the prayers of those who cry to Him in their trouble, and showing, by many illustrations, how "He bringeth them out of their distresses," the Psalmist concludes with these comforting words: "Whoso is wise and will observe these things, even they shall understand the loving kindness of the Lord."

O, I beg those who have never " observed these things" before, to make haste to do so, that they may understand how excellent is the loving kindness of Jehovah, and how His "faithfulness reacheth unto the clouds."

Filled then with the praises of our Lord, and lost in His love, we shall all be one in Him; we shall "be planted in the house of the Lord" and "shall flourish in the courts of our God." One of the most beautiful things in this life of faith, and utter dependence on our Father, is that all who come into it learn to recognize their fellow-Christians in the "unity of the faith." — Eph. 4:13. A gentleman .said to me not long ago: "I believe that the Church of the present time is in ruins. Christians nowadays are Methodists, Presbyterians, Baptists, Episcopalians, etc., and they are not united as the Church of Christ."

But, in the midst of that seeming division, there stands one glorious, triumphant body, composed of the faithful of all denominations, who know "one Lord, one faith, one baptism, one God and Father of all" (Eph. 4:5, 6), and who "have been all made to drink into one Spirit." — 1 Cor. 12:13.

These "fitly joined together" in love "are the body of Christ, and members in particular; "these are the true "Church Militant;" the "armies of the living God" who are "strong in the Lord and in the power of His night." Among themselves they "keep the unity of the Spirit in the bond of peace; " but with the enemy of souls they are fighting " the good fight of faith." They have "put on the whole armour of God," that they "may be able to stand against the wiles of the devil."

"Stand, therefore, having your loins girt about with truth, and having on the breastplate of righteouness; and your feet shod with the preparation of the gospel of peace; above all, taking the shield of faith, wherewith ye shall be able to quench all the fiery darts of the wicked. And take the helmet of salvation, and the sword of the Spirit, which is the word of God." — Eph. 6:14-17.

"Watch ye, stand fast in the faith, quit you like men, be strong." — 1 Cor. 16:13. "And the multitudes of them that believed were of one heart and of one soul." — Acts 4:32.

My dear friends, let us breathe a prayer together before we part: "And now, Lord grant unto thy servants, that with all boldness they may speak Thy word, by stretching forth Thine hand to heal; and that signs and wonders may be done by the Name of The holy child Jesus." — Acts 4:29,30.

THE END.